Becoming:
"The One"

*Live a life
of inspiration!*

♡

Bonnie

Becoming:
"The One"

✦

A guide to discovering your true soul mate within

Bonnie Bruderer

iUniverse, Inc.
New York Lincoln Shanghai

Becoming: "The One"
A guide to discovering your true soul mate within

iUniverse books may be ordered through booksellers or by contacting:

iUniverse
2021 Pine Lake Road, Suite 100
Lincoln, NE 68512
www.iuniverse.com
1-800-Authors (1-800-288-4677)

ISBN-13: 978-0-595-37863-0 (pbk)
ISBN-13: 978-0-595-82236-2 (ebk)
ISBN-10: 0-595-37863-3 (pbk)
ISBN-10: 0-595-82236-3 (ebk)

Printed in the United States of America

To all of my amazing girlfriends,

You know who you are.

Thank you for all of your laughter, fun, joy, tears and love!

Contents

Introduction

If you have picked up this book, it is because you have a need. You may feel as though there is something missing in your life. This may be a relationship, an ideal job, or something that you can't quite put your finger on. Rest assured, this book can help. I can guide you into unlocking the secret that will lead you to attracting anything you desire into your life. In turn, you will embark on an amazing journey of self-discovery and learn how to create abundance. The only thing required from you is an open mind and to be true to yourself.

I want to acknowledge you for being brave enough to pick up this book, and I commend you for taking the steps toward self-discovery and your true desires.

This book will work for you because it is truth. Without truth, there is no chance for any type of a successful relationship. Not with yourself, and certainly not with anyone else.

From countless learning experiences to years of heartbreak, through numerous blind dates and hilarious dating encounters, I will share situations that will leave you laughing hysterically and situations that, if you can relate, will have you crying profusely. Through my learning experiences, I can teach you what you need to know. I will share my journey with you as you embark upon your own. You will find that you have everything you need to find your true soul mate within, as well as anything else you desire in life. Simple as that…Enjoy!

1

The Journey

The amazing gift you will receive as you embark on your soul-mate journey is the knowledge that everything you need lies within.

I was a bit of an unusual child. I was born with a passion for self-growth. Even as a small child, I remember being the one people came to for advice. If someone was thrown out of the sandbox and upset about it, I was the one who befriended them and explained that it had nothing to do with them and everything to do with the bully. I had somewhat of a sixth sense.

As a child, I remember my mother taking my brother and I to the library. After all of the other children had gone in to hear the story hour and select their children's book to bring home for the week, I would sneak into the self-help section of the library. I can still remember the feeling. Even as a kid, I knew that the words *self-help* had some sort of a stigma attached to them. I wasn't really sure if I was even allowed to read these books; some of them included grown-up words like *intimacy* and *relationships*. Luckily, the card catalog was strategically placed so that you couldn't see the self-help section from the kiddy corner, so I knew I was in the clear, at least for a while. I read books on everything from intimate relationships and happiness to discovering yourself. I was simply fascinated with the content.

Fast-forward twenty-five years. In that time, I have gained a wealth of knowledge and a passion for helping women discover themselves and learn how to attract virtually anything they desire in their lives. For the last four years, I have had a job working for one of the world's leading experts on personal development seminars. My job involves traveling around the world as a coach and mentor to the people who attend these seminars.

It took me a lot longer than most to learn these lessons and to learn that you must love yourself first, before anyone else can love you. I remember in my earlier years of dating, my mother and my aunt told me to always be myself. It sounded so simple and so obvious. It wasn't. It took me thirty years, tens of thousands of dollars spent on self-discovery and motivational seminars, a month spent at an ashram in meditation with swamis, countless visits to a therapist, hundreds of books, different churches and religious organizations, and many failed relationships to learn these lessons. The funny thing is that pretty much everyone was saying the same thing. The swami said the secret is to "know thyself." The therapist said to know who you really are. The motivational speakers said to know your purpose. But I did not understand any of this on the level that was necessary to be successful. All I knew was that I desperately wanted a sense of inner contentment. I wanted to find romance and love. I wanted to be fulfilled in my career. I seemed to fail no matter how hard I tried. Then I realized something. Relationships are not as complicated as we women make them seem. If you can discover who you are and what you truly stand for, you can have your true soul mate whenever you desire. The secret is to become your own soul mate. As we embark on this journey, you will discover things you never knew about yourself.

The first part of realizing who you are is learning what is truly important to you. What do you really value in your life? What will you absolutely not stand for, and what is essential for you to be happy in your life and in your relationships?

The first thing you should do is get a notebook that you can use throughout these exercises. Start the notebook by making a list of everything in your life that is important. Be as detailed and specific as you like. Write down everything that makes you happy, everything that you enjoy, and everything that you like about yourself. Decide what you absolutely need to be fulfilled as well as what you need to do away with to be the woman you were born to be.

The list is the easy part. Now, look over your list and highlight all of the qualities you already possess. Most likely, you will realize that you do not practice or exemplify some of the areas that are most important to you. Highlight these areas; they will be your opportunities for improvement and growth. It is critical that you be brutally honest with yourself because these are qualities that, once developed, will help you to become your true self and be open to attracting anything you desire. These qualities will help bring you a sense of inner peace and fulfillment.

So many times in life, we don't realize what isn't working. We try to rearrange things in our lives and to look externally to find happiness. Many of us will enter into new relationships or careers only to achieve the same result each time. We continue to blame our failures on another person or on our job, even when it was us doing the choosing. For example, as women, we may spend much of our time waiting for a man to send us roses rather than planting and cultivating our own rose garden. With our own garden, we can have gorgeous roses any time we want.

It is important to have a clear, concise vision of who you truly are. You can refer to this as your "soul sentence." Once you have created this sentence, live by it. I developed mine at a seminar about eight years ago. I can honestly say that I live by it and make sure that all of my decisions and choices support it. I am happy to share it with you to give you an idea of how to get started with yours: "The purpose of my life is to have passion, health, and happiness, and to spread love and joy to others."

It is very helpful to become intimately familiar with your soul sentence. Once you have designed it, write it out on some fun paper and decorate it. Place a copy on your bathroom mirror and another copy on your desk at work. Repeat it to yourself throughout the day. Repeat it while you are working out or going for a walk. Keep repeating it to yourself until it becomes a part of who you are. Once you begin to focus on your soul statement and who you truly are, I guarantee that you will start to see changes in all areas of your life.

The following chapters will guide you through discovering the most important areas of your life. These areas, when mastered, will help you create abundance in all areas of your life. Their mastery will guide you into creating ultimate love and acceptance for yourself. Through the journey, you will learn to enrich all of your relationships and attract anything you desire. The most important part is to trust in the process and enjoy the journey, as you learn and discover new things about yourself.

Many practices can lead to this openness and guided state. There will many exercises given to you in a very short period, in hopes that you will try some of them on and figure out which practices will work best with your lifestyle. Many different paths are open to you, and I am happy to share mine with you, to help you learn. Keep in mind that these are just a few of the tools that worked for me. I encourage you to find out what will work for you. There are thousands of activities that can contribute to an open heart and openness to learning.

Some days, I feel as though every single word spoken by every person I come across is a lesson that I need to hear. Whether it is from a taxi driver, the grocery store cashier, or a wise sage, the lesson is there. Feeling as if you are learning from everyone that crosses your path is an excellent place to be, but it took me many years to learn how to be in this place.

Here are some of the tools that have helped me on my journey:

- *Journaling.* I think every girl at some stage in her life has had a small pink book with a gold lock and the word *Diary* on it. You may have kept yours on the top shelf of your closet or under your bed—a book filled with all of the thoughts and secrets that you didn't want to share with your friends or siblings. I didn't realize when I was young how powerful a tool journaling was and how it contributed to my growth. It can also be extremely therapeutic and an excellent form of release.

  My best friend has strict orders to destroy my journals should anything tragic ever happen to me. I use the tool of journaling to work through all the problems that I do not want to burden anyone else with. For me, my journal serves as the perfect place to vent, a place to safely divulge all of my secrets, challenges, and fears—a sacred place where I can be as negative or as un-resourceful as I need to be without being judged. By writing my problems down on paper, I end up finding my own solutions. I am able to get out all of my anger and frustration, and by the end of my writing, I am able to see the positive aspects of the situation and create new solutions. If I had chosen just to share my frustration and anger with a girlfriend, all I would have done is added fuel to the fire and not solved anything. Journaling is also an excellent tool to write out everything you desire in your life. It is a safe place to create your wish lists or to document all of your blessings and write about the things you are grateful for.

- *Meditation.* Meditation is another excellent tool to help you solve problems throughout your journey. You can meditate many different ways, and there is surely no right or wrong way to meditate. Meditation can be as simple as sitting quietly and clearing your mind. Once all of the noise and clutter is gone, many times answers to pending questions miraculously appear. This is also a practice that you can use anywhere. Once you learn the skill of quieting your mind, you can access this skill while driving or while waiting in line at the supermarket. For some people, it helps to join an organized group to learn how to meditate. A great way to find a meditation group is to check into any local Buddhist temple or Eastern religious organization. There are also many great audio and video programs that you can purchase for use at home.

- *Massage.* I believe that all of your experiences and emotions are stored somewhere in your body. These experiences and emotions might be holding you back from your dreams and desires. Massage is an excellent way to calm and quiet your mind to allow these feelings to surface so you can process them. There are a few things you should consider when choosing a massage therapist. First, find someone with whom you are comfortable. Massage is an extremely intimate process, and, to get the maximum benefits from your experience, it is important that you feel safe and comfortable. Second, find a massage therapist who has similar beliefs as you, who also believes that emotions and experiences are stored within your body and can be released through massage. It is not uncommon to experience a period of intense emotion or crying for a period of time after a massage. This happens because you are releasing and processing stored emotions at a deep cellular level. Once you experience the emotion or situation, you are able to move forward with what you want in your life. If you do not process these emotions, they can create stumbling blocks for you when you enter into relationships.

- *Yoga.* Like massage, yoga is designed to release stress and tension that can be stored throughout your body. Yoga is a series of exercises that will work your entire body. It is common to start yoga with a meditation or a series of breathing exercises, which complements your meditation practice. There are many modalities of yoga to choose from, so you will have to decide which type and level is best for you. I recommend a gentle-type modality, such as hatha yoga. It is also important to find a studio and instructor with whom you feel very comfortable and who shares your beliefs. These days, there are multiple yoga studios in many communities. If you are having trouble finding a studio specifically for yoga, most gyms offer a variety of classes.

- *Exercise.* Exercise can also be used as a tool to help you on your path to self-discovery. In addition to the overall health benefits and the great feeling exercise will give you, it can also be meditative. My sport of choice is the triathlon. I discovered the triathlon about eight years ago and immediately realized how valuable it is for helping me process thoughts and emotions. I have resolved numerous challenges while training for races. In fact, I thought of the concept for this book while training for an Ironman triathlon. I was out on the bike for seven hours that day. There were periods of that bike ride that were so tough, I needed anything I could find to get the ride off my mind. I found that if I could focus on something else, I could ride the hills better. After thinking about what I valued in my life and what I wanted to share with other women, the idea for this book came to my mind.

Incidentally, I discovered that whenever you have challenges in life, focusing on something else helps you take your mind off the problem until you discover a solution. Another great exercise to do when you're looking for answers is swimming. Once you get into the rhythm of your swim workout, it is easy to focus on a mantra or meditate. While I was training for some of the races I have competed in, I would swim at the pool every evening. I found that no matter what state of mind I went to the pool in, once I was finished, I felt amazing and had a clear head. Running is also extremely therapeutic. I like to use my time running to repeat a mantra. For example, if I am in need of a certain attribute in my life, I will repeat that attribute over and over again. If I have a presentation coming up that I am nervous about, I will repeat, "I am knowledgeable, powerful, and confident" throughout my entire run. I find that once I am finished repeating the mantra, these traits just seem to come naturally to me.

- *Peers.* Your peer group is also essential to your success along your journey. It is important that you surround yourself with people who are like-minded and who will support you during your different stages of learning. On the other hand, you may find that there are certain friends or family members whom you need to distance yourself from during this process. At the peak of my self-discovery, I actually decided to move away entirely from my current lifestyle, peer group, and family. I moved from San Francisco where I had grown up to San Diego. For me this change was necessary, not because my friends and family were bad people—quite the contrary. Rather, it was because I needed space to grow. During the time I decided to move, all of my girlfriends were getting married. That may seem like an exaggeration to you, but I can tell you I went to twelve weddings that summer. Along with that, for each wedding there were multiple showers, bachelorette parties, and engagement parties. This was a huge wound for me. I wanted to be at this same place in life, getting married and starting my life with someone. The entire focus of my peer group during those two years was weddings. About the same time I had just ended a three-year relationship, so I was also balancing the change and grief associated with that. I knew, at that point in my life, I was on an accelerated growth path and I needed to be true to myself and follow this path.

My situation at the time presented a few problems. First, it constantly reminded me that I didn't have what I wanted in my life and that, it seemed, everyone else had exactly what they wanted Second, I didn't feel like I could relate to where my friends were in life. All of their focus was on weddings and starting the next phase of their lives, as it well should have been. I felt alone and unable to relate to them, and vice versa. A third challenge this situation presented was to examine my current situation as well as the choices that I had made in the past that didn't give me the results I wanted. A big part of this process was to examine my belief system and how I grew up. I found it difficult to be in such close proximity to my family while I was going through this process; when you are close to your family, it is very easy to slip into roles that you played in your family during your younger years rather than being the person you are today.

I moved to San Diego without knowing a single person there. Everything was new to me. I didn't have a single friend with whom to hang out. My job was new; my studio was new. It took me about six months before I had any semblance of a social life. I would go home from work at 6 o'clock each night and read, process, and design what I truly wanted out of my life. What was great about it was that I was able to learn what was important to me and what I needed in friendships. I was able to meet people who were interested in the same activities as I was. I was able to form the deep, intimate friendships that I longed for. I remained very close with my friends from San Francisco, but at the same time had this new, different level of life for myself. I was able to design my dream life and have it full of everything that made me happy and fulfilled. I had gone from doing the same thing every weekend that I had done all through college to having a life full of growth, challenge, and intimacy. You may not need to go to the same extremes I did, but I wanted to share my story with you to let you know it is possible to create a rewarding, supportive, loving peer group even in a new environment.

- *Daily prayers and gratitude.* The last tool I will share with you in this chapter is the practice of daily prayers and gratitude, something that has helped me immensely. This is a simple practice of stating what you are grateful for each day, as well as soliciting what you would like to manifest into your life. It does not matter what your religious beliefs are: this is a practice that anyone can use. Each morning I like to go sit outside, preferably to the beach, and state out loud everything and everyone I am grateful for in my life. I find that even on days when I feel as though nothing is going right, my gratitude list goes on and on. This activity in itself makes me feel great, and usually I forget about what was bothering me. My intentions are done exactly the same way; I ask my higher power to bless me with whatever it is I feel I need, such as strength or compassion. I think you will find that just identifying what it is you need, as well as focusing on it, usually attracts these things into your life. I also recommend using this time to ask your higher power to bless anyone in your life with whatever it is they desire.

Again, I have just shared a handful of the tools that I have found valuable on my path toward self-growth. I know that these will be useful for you. All of these tools are designed to help you gain clarity and to realize what you truly desire in your life. Enjoy them!

2

Understanding Your History

Although your past does not necessarily predict your future, understanding it can truly set you free.

It is early one Saturday morning, and I am nestled cozily into my fluffy down comforter on my bed when all of a sudden I have the eerie feeling that someone is watching me. I open my eyes to find a pair of big brown eyes only inches from my face. Along with those big brown eyes are a huge muzzle and a ball of fluffy black and white fur. It is my best friend at the time, a thirteen-year-old English springer spaniel named Flame. As she senses me starting to awaken, she whines, letting me know she is eager to go outside. I roll over and nudge Brad, my live-in boyfriend at the time. He grunts and rolls over to the opposite side of the bed, taking the majority of the covers and the warmth with him. Like most other household chores at this time, Flame has somehow become entirely my responsibility. I roll my eyes and let out a sigh. I am not overly excited to embark into the foggy predawn morning, but the truth is that I have fallen in love with this little ball of fur and would pretty much do anything to make sure she is taken care of.

I kick around the pile of clothes lying on the floor and find some oversized sweats that will do the job. Flame, now pacing wildly, is in front of the door, whining profusely. I scurry to find the leash and a plastic bag and we are ready to go. She begins to run down the stairs, turning about every third one and doubling back to make sure that I am coming; she jumps up to give me some love. I think to myself, "Animals are such simple creatures." Flame possesses the excitement of an eight-year-old on her first trip to Disneyland. In reality, all we are doing is going outside so she can go to the bathroom. But her warmth and vitality leaves me wanting more in my own life. Isn't it every woman's dream to find a man who will love her as much and as unconditionally as a dog does? This little bundle of joy sleeps in front of the door all day after I leave, just awaiting my return. Don't we all deserve to have someone who listens for our footsteps coming home after a long day at work, to find someone bounding with joy, pouncing on us, and giving us big slobbering kisses for the simple fact that we are home? Someone whose feet (all four of them!) leave the ground with all-consuming excitement when we walk through the door?

Then reality hits. Flame does her business and begins to nudge me in the knee with her damp nose. She instantly breaks my daydream.

As we walk back up the stairs and head toward the door, I am overcome with a chilling thought that stops me in my tracks. Could it possibly be? Is it really? Please tell me it isn't Saturday. Saturdays for us were better known as "break-up Saturdays."

Of course, everything was perfect in the beginning of our relationship. It was all hugs, kisses, and roses. Lately I could not believe that we had ever gotten along. Brad had been traveling a great deal with his job. He would leave town on Monday night and return on Thursday or Friday. Usually he would return too exhausted for anything more than collapsing on the couch and spending the entire evening ignoring me and driving the remote control. That brings me to "break-up Saturday." I called it this because that is usually when things would go down. Brad was exhausted from the trials and tribulations of life on the road. Me, well, I was pretty much just tired of being alone most of the time, ignored when I wasn't, and miserable because I felt totally unfulfilled in the relationship. It wasn't meeting any of my needs and it was increasingly difficult to even get along.

We would attempt to start the day out right, but within the first hour of conversation, tensions would come to a head and catastrophe would be on the horizon.

Brad would ask me if I wanted to take Flame down to the Stratford Café for breakfast. It was a quaint little breakfast spot that was within walking distance from where we lived. Somewhere between washing my face and getting dressed in my Saturday cozies, things would take a turn for the worse.

Some Saturdays started with an accusation of jealously on his part or my ever-favorite line, "I feel like we are drifting apart." The big whammy always came when Brad would tell me that he didn't think he would be able to meet my needs. Regardless of how it started, the results were usually the same: a morning and early afternoon filled with ineffective communication strategies. Tears would stream down my face, and anger and sadness would well up inside me as I desperately tried to communicate my needs and the fact that I didn't feel appreciated or loved. As human nature predicts, when a male hears those words, it pushes him even further away, thus leaving the woman even sadder, alone, and in fear of losing the relationship. Usually by midmorning, he would storm out, slam the door, stomp down the stairs, and speed off in his overpriced sports car.

I would sometimes spend the better part of the morning curled up in the fetal position bawling my eyes out. I would wonder how I could have ever gotten myself into this situation. Brad had convinced me to move in with him, even though I swore I would never do that before being married. He told me to trust him that he would support me while I went back to school, even though I wanted to support myself. Flame, faithfully by my side, would nestle right up next to me to lick away the tears with her big sloppy kisses. I would spend the rest of the afternoon building myself up and reminding myself of all the reasons I was better than this and that I deserved someone better. This was usually done kneeling over the apartments-for-rent section of the newspaper with a highlighter in hand, looking for an apartment I could afford. I was truly miserable and felt trapped; I really wasn't in a position to be able to support myself.

About four in the afternoon, Brad would come home with a look of defeat and two large bags full of take-out food from the local BBQ restaurant. He would grumble some half-hearted apology and tell me that he wanted this to work out. This was the pattern, and it went on for months. I let it go on because I was desperate to make the relationship work and I didn't realize why I was ending up in this situation time and again.

If this story or a version of it sounds remotely familiar to you or someone you know, you need to read this chapter. If you are caught in a rut and experiencing a dysfunctional pattern in your relationship, it is most likely due to your past, and how you grew up. So many times in life, we are unaware that the damaging choices we make are a result of experiences from our childhood. Until we truly understand these past experiences and the reasons we are reliving the pain in our current relationships, we don't have any chance of moving forward. We may make choices that are seemingly different or choose a relationship that looks like it comes in a different package. But, lo and behold, the results are always the same.

For example, if you grew up in a family with an alcoholic, you have lived with painful and dysfunctional dynamics. If you were taught at a young age to lie to cover up embarrassing or potentially harmful behavior, this may seem natural for you. You may choose partners that you can't trust or depend on. I work with so many women that tell me they can't believe that their partner is an alcoholic and doesn't treat them right. They can't believe this happened to them because they spent so many of their childhood years dealing with this same behavior from their father. Basing your life on experiences from your childhood is sometimes almost an unconscious decision, and if you don't realize that you follow these patterns, you may just chalk it up to bad luck.

You may not have even grown up with an awareness of how your history is showing up in your present life. If you are unaware, it is almost certain that you will make choices that put you in similar situations with similar dynamics. This is because the behavior is familiar to you and, although at times it can be extremely painful, it is almost comfortable.

If you are aware of the pattern but lack the knowledge of how to move through it, you may find yourself choosing the same set of problems in a different package. You may choose someone that does not drink because you have a great deal of pain associated with that from your past; however, you may choose a workaholic that treats you in very similar ways.

To illustrate this, I will share an example from my own relationship history. I grew up in a family where one of my parents had a drinking problem. This produced many difficult situations where I was forced to tolerate behavior that was unacceptable. Some of this included hearing things that should not have been said, such as broken promises and continuous lies to cover up problems that drinking created, lack of trust, and also constant disappointment. In my family, I ended up being the caretaker and taking responsibility for things that should have been taken care of by my parent. I also had a strong desire to make sure everyone around me was as happy as possible given the set of circumstances. Because of the difficult situations I faced, I grew up to be someone who always wanted to help people.

Because I wanted to help others, I often didn't follow my own dreams or desires and instead gave to everyone else. I was constantly exhausted, but I was good at it. Later in life, when I began to have relationships, guess what type of companions I chose? I chose the people who needed fixing; that was my strength. I went with the obvious choices at first, the people who had the same patterns that I was used to. My first boyfriend had a major drinking problem. Because of his drinking, what also showed up in our relationship were broken promises, lack of trust, and constant disappointment. What a surprise! This was where I was comfortable. Although I was truly miserable in the relationship, at least I knew how to deal with what was showing up.

At this point in my progression, I thought I had learned my lesson. My next few boyfriends were guys who had passions in their lives that were much more important to them than our relationship. The next was a professional golfer, and the next a workaholic. Although I thought I was making good choices, I was actually choosing people who would treat me the same way I had been treated in previous relationships, as they put their work and their sport first. With both of these relationships, guess what showed up? Broken promises, lack of trust, and constant disappointment.

When we are unaware of our patterns, we are sure to keep repeating them. In all of the above scenarios, there is a common theme. There was something dysfunctional in each of these people that prevented them from being fully present and able to embark on the level of intimacy that I desired.

This is why it is crucial that you understand what you are looking for as well as what your relationship patterns are. Relationships are such an important part of life. The most important relationship is the one you have with yourself. Once you realize why you surround yourself with the types of relationships you are in, you can make the necessary changes and have lasting fulfillment. This can work in all areas of your life, including intimate relationships as well as relationships with family members or coworkers.

Here are a few exercises that you can do to find out what your patterns are. First, take your notebook and write down your brief childhood story. List important facts such as whether your parents were married or divorced. Write down everything you loved about your childhood and everything that you didn't like. Make sure to include anything important such as major illnesses, deaths in the family, problems with alcohol or depression, and so on. Once you have created your list, study it and see if there is anything there that surprises you. Take a few moments to discover whether anything clearly contributes to the decisions you have made about your relationships.

My guess is that many things on this list will surprise you. Many people don't take the time to identify their past and what could be causing challenges in their current lives. I am always amazed when I coach people who can't figure out why they are terrified to settle down in their current relationship. Usually, after some brief examination, we discover a major event such as a divorce that left them scared. The fear of repeating this pattern and causing pain to your own family can prevents you from being able to enter into a long-term committed relationship. Once these patterns are identified and the pain is released, it allows room for you to foster new options.

Once you have spent some time on the list above, it is time to delve into your own relationship history. This can be a pleasant stroll down memory lane for some and a nightmare for others. As with all of the other exercises, it is imperative to be brutally honest with yourself. Again, take your notebook and write down your relationship history. Start from the very beginning. Write down your very first memory of having feelings for the opposite sex. The early memories can be a huge clue to identifying your relationship choices. For example, I remember when I was in first grade, the boys would play a game called "cutie kissers." I remember watching all of the popular girls being kissed by the boys who played. I was so afraid that nobody would kiss me. I can remember clearly the day that the most popular boy in school "cutie kissed" me during recess and I finally felt as though I fit in. These early memories can tell us a great deal about our confidence, how we feel about rejection, and much more.

Now that you have your early memories down, begin to write out all of your serious relationships in sequential order. Write out the amount of time you were in the relationship, how it started, and how it ended. Write out as many details as you can remember about how confident or insecure you felt. What did you like about this relationship and what didn't you like? The process of identifying your different experiences in relationships will help you to identify what patterns you are running. You will discover both positive and negative patterns in this exercise. Obviously, you want to continue to use what helped you create great relationships and work through the areas that created poor relationships.

If you are at all like me, you will find that writing your relationship history can be a bit depressing; there may be obvious destructive patterns that you have repeated over and over again. Again, I will refer you to the example of the alcoholic and the workaholic. The good news is that awareness is the first step in changing your patterns. Once you are aware of the choices you have made and why you made them, you can make different choices in the future. When you identify the reasons you made poor choices, make sure to write down what you have learned from each of these experiences and why you will not make those same choices again.

Now that you have identified why you made the choices you made and why you will not repeat them, you are on your way to making the perfect choice in your future relationships. More importantly, you are on the path to creating a successful and loving relationship with yourself.

3

Acceptance

**We must fully love and accept ourselves before we
will allow others to accept us.**

The years between twenty-three and twenty-six were pretty crazy for me. I had
somehow managed to land myself in a relationship with an extremely wealthy
man with a jet-set lifestyle. At twenty-three years old, who wouldn't be awed with
a fleet of yachts, helicopters, motorized cable cars, jet skis, and backstage passes
for pretty much any band you wanted to see? Of course, it was never my intention to attract someone like this, nor did any of his stuff really matter to me. But
that was where I was.

Let's start a few years back when I was sixteen years old, working at a wedding
show. There I was with my big perm and my even bigger bangs. I was all gussied
up for the occasion in my paisley black, silver, and turquoise sweater set. The
ridiculous part was that it had matching pants, and I was wearing them. The
pants were made out of the exact weave and colors as the sweater. The set itself
was a hand-me-down from my older cousin—that fact in itself told me it was
cool.

I wobbled across the crowded floor in my suede black heels that matched the
outfit. The heels seemed to have a mind of their own as I made my way across the
long cement showroom floor. My destination was the King's Kustom Tuxedo
booth. I walked with an air of confidence because I felt honored to have this
opportunity to work at the expo. I was only able to put in sixteen hours a week at
the job, as I was only a junior in high school. To have been selected over all of the
full-time women who worked at the shop was a huge honor.

As the day wore on, I busily dressed and straightened the outfits on the man-
nequins in our booth. I took special care to ensure that their bright-colored bow
ties were perfectly aligned. As I was adjusting a certain metallic purple cummer-
bund, out of nowhere, this amazingly gorgeous guy caught my eye. It was as if, at
that instant, everything else stopped around me and my surroundings became a

blur (imagine "Dream Weaver" playing loudly in my head). I couldn't help but stare at him. There was Tom. He was wearing a sharp black tuxedo and a chauffeur's hat. We looked at each other for a brief second and I saw a diamond-like twinkle in his eye. Come to think of it now, it could have been the fluorescent lighting reflecting off my mouthful of braces, but being the dreamer I am, this is how I chose to remember the encounter. I had an instant crush. I needed to somehow find a way to meet this gorgeous man. In that instant, I noticed my manager going over to speak with him. This would be my big break, I thought. When my manager did introduce him, I couldn't conjure up anything dazzling to say, so I just returned to my booth, somewhat hormone-crazed and stunned. For the rest of the afternoon, I continued with my staring campaign. I noticed there were more women in his booth for his business, all day than in a Nordstrom's dressing room during the semiannual sale.

Fast-forward eight years. I am twenty-three years old, thankfully free from the braces and matching paisley sweater set. I was in my first career job, as an event planner. The team of girls that I worked with had been invited to a "Cable Car Bar Crawl." When the faxed invitation had arrived at our office, I had mentioned in passing that I knew the guy who was throwing it, but since I was the new girl, nobody seemed to pay much attention to me. The event consisted of approximately fifty event planners from around San Francisco. We started at a famous bar on the Embarcadero called Pier 23. It was our first stop, and I saw Tom. I immediately had the same sensation I had experienced eight years earlier at our chance meeting at the wedding show. I had my over-rambunctious coworker (you know the type—the ones with no fear) summons him. With a big grin, she said, "Do you remember this girl?" I giggled, as he looked deeply into my eyes and said, "Of course. I met you years ago at an expo." I was delighted and a bit shocked that he had remembered me at all, but he did. That was the start of what proved to be a great reintroduction, an intense evening, and a three-year relationship.

I knew right away that Tom was different from me and all of my friends. We were all just straight out of college. He was older, sophisticated, wealthy, and successful. I immediately found it a bit difficult to be myself around him. I am not sure to this day just exactly who I was being, but it wasn't quite myself. I felt an immediate pressure to be impressive. It was almost as though I was a magnified, over exaggerated version of myself, always showing my strengths and never my weaknesses.

As the relationship grew, I learned two things. Number one, I was absolutely terrified of losing someone in a relationship. Number two, Tom had figured this out, and he held it over me every chance he had to ensure that I acted exactly the way he wanted me to. I was a Stepford me. There were noticeable differences that became apparent right away. The most prominent was our lifestyle differences. Tom ran a very successful company. It was the type of company that demanded long hours and little chance for quality time for a relationship. He also had a belief that people don't need as much sleep as most everyone else seems to think.

The first few months, I was consumed by the romance and the typical excitement that comes with a new relationship. I would come home from work on cloud nine. Later in the evenings, Tom would call, and I would primp myself as if I were starting the day from scratch. I would head over to his house for a late-night rendezvous. This was all too exciting at first. However, sleep deprivation soon caught up with me and I found myself having miserable mornings at work. I soon began to drink coffee and found myself, more mornings than not, skipping my morning workout that used to make me feel so great. The coffee was definitely a new thing for me, and I soon found myself up to a Venti at Starbucks each morning, just to get myself through the day. Health had always been so important to me, so it seemed strange that I found myself with these newly developed habits.

Months into the relationship, the lack of sleep began to border on ridiculous. I was so desperate for Tom to accept me that I would go to any lengths imaginable just to gain his approval. I would come home from work and immediately sleep for a few hours to make up for the lack of sleep the night before. At around nine o'clock in the evening, I would get up, shower, apply make-up, style my hair, and await his evening phone call, as his workday was wrapping up. I would pretend that this is just how I was, that I was always up this late just hanging out and it would be no problem to come over. I kept up this charade for many months, and it began to carry over into other areas of the relationship.

I became terrified of being who I truly was, in fear that I wouldn't be good enough and Tom would dump me. The truth was I was an attractive, fun, bubbly, kind, compassionate, and honest person (one who normally would go to bed at a decent hour of the night, and who had feelings and opinions). I lived with the constant fear of not being accepted. The truth was, I wasn't yet aware that someone could love, accept, and appreciate me for who I truly was. You see, I hadn't yet learned to truly accept myself.

I remember the crisp autumn day when the situation with Tom began to come to a halt. I was running around the streets of San Francisco like an errand demon at Tom's beck and call. I was supposed to have been home half an hour before that to meet my best friend for happy hour. I had not yet completed all of

Tom's errands, but I needed to hurry to meet her, as Tom had booked us for something later that evening.

I ran into a few challenges that day, as you often do with running errands in a big city, and I was exhausted. I was walking up the steep grade of Clement Street, overwhelmed with the dry cleaning, the laptop bag, the purse, and the nine other things I had to carry. My roommate was out front waiting for me. As soon as we caught each other's glance, I began to sob. "I just can't take it anymore," I exclaimed as tears flowed down my face. As I entered the house I proceeded to throw a toddler-style temper tantrum as the dry cleaning, laptop, and everything else went crashing to the floor. Luckily, I had an amazing best friend and she knew exactly what to do. She grabbed the ever-fateful "box of wine" from the fridge. This was the wine never to be drunk. It had been there for at least a year, left behind from one of the many theme parties we had thrown, and it was most likely brought there in the first place as a joke. It was all we had, and it would have to do. We plunked ourselves down on the couch with our box of wine and our two glasses, and she listened intently as I clamored on about how I was exhausted and didn't know who I was anymore. I told her I didn't have the energy to be this perfect person anymore and that I just wanted to be myself. I also knew in that moment that as frustrated as I was, I was also scared of not being accepted for who I was.

This lesson of self-acceptance is one that took me a long time and many relationships to learn. Acceptance is an essential component of any relationship. It is critically important for you to accept yourself before you can accept anyone else.

Acceptance is learning, understanding, and realizing that you are a gift worth receiving, and accepting that gift. This means not always striving to be someone else or always striving to be better. Don't misunderstand me, it is admirable to embark on the path of self-growth and to strive to become more. What most people miss is that it is important to accept where you are now, so you are truly striving to become better, rather than striving to become someone else.

Acceptance is being able to love and validate who you are, even the parts you would eventually like to change. By accepting each of these parts of ourselves, even the parts we want to change, it allows us to truly open up and accept others as they are. This creates and cultivates a lasting love.

There are many reasons why acceptance is often difficult. For example, if you are dealing with self-esteem or self-worth issues, accepting yourself can be difficult. You may have the underlying desire to change yourself, but you are afraid that if you were to accept yourself as you already are, you would not be motivated to change. This is simply not true: letting go of our self-judgments and accepting ourselves allows us even more power to make the changes we desire. Acceptance completely eliminates fear, the fear of trying to make a change, but failing.

There are a few factors I would encourage you to look at when dealing with the topic of acceptance:

- First, get to know yourself and what you believe in. Ask yourself these questions: Who are you? What is important to you in your life? What do you believe? These may seem like simple questions, but you would be surprised at how many people have never asked them of themselves.

- Second, check your integrity level. How honest are you currently with yourself? How honest are you with others? Do you always communicate your true desires and wants to others? What do you believe to be true about yourself? What are your goals? Do you honestly believe you can achieve your goals? Do you honestly feel you deserve them?

- Third, look at your current acceptance level. Do you openly accept yourself? Do you like yourself? Do you accept others? What characteristics do you like about yourself? Which ones would you like to change? Do you see a reason to love and accept yourself the way you are right now?

- Fourth, embrace the fact that you are doing the best you can with what you have. I believe that people sincerely do the best they can with the knowledge and resources they have at the time, especially when they are honest, open, and accepting of themselves and others. Giving yourself a break and acknowledging yourself for doing a great job now is acceptance. Let go of desires to do better, be better, or be different. This will allow you to see others in the same light, enriching all of your existing relationships as well as future relationships.

- Fifth, let go of any guilt that you may have. Guilt is a useless emotion. As far as love and acceptance are concerned, the emotion of guilt really holds no place. If you truly feel guilty about something, it is usually because you are not comfortable with a choice you have made. Instead of feeling the useless emotion of guilt, learn from the choices you have made and make different choices in the future.

- Finally, understand your motivations. Understand your likes and dislikes about yourself. A desire to constantly grow, learn, and improve is honorable. Just make sure that you are simultaneously accepting and loving all areas of yourself, even the areas you want to change.

Relationships where one or both parties aren't truly able to be themselves are destined for failure. You will quickly realize that you can't live inauthentically. Your energy is so much better served if people are allowed to be themselves and love and grow together for who they are. Once you are able to master acceptance, you are well on your way to finding enriching, fulfilling relationships with all.

4

Progression Power

Each relationship is a learning experience and a growth opportunity.

There is nothing like a cold, crisp San Francisco afternoon. With the fog gently rolling in and the faint smell of sea in the air, Ashley and I were off on our afternoon walk. We needed to compensate for all of the brownies we had devoured that afternoon. As we speed-walked the ever-increasing grade of California Street, our arms flailed madly in front of us. "You know Tom is going to ask you to marry him on your trip to Mexico next week," Ashley proclaimed.

Remember, I'm the girl who never gets upset with anyone and rarely shows any kind of negative emotion, but I stopped dead in my tracks and gave Ash a look of terror. "Why would you tell me that?" I yelled. "Number one, it is probably not true, and number two, you could have very well ruined one of the single most important moments of my life!"

Quickly fumbling for something to say, anything at all, she told me, "That's what he told my fiancé, when we were out on the boat Sunday, enjoying the sun and playing backgammon."

I was so furious with her, I could hardly believe it. Not wanting to ever have any tension between my friends and me, I chose not to continue the conversation, and instead I let it stew inside as we continued up California Street.

Looking back, I have to admit, although angry at the potential of blowing the surprise of the engagement, I was bubbling inside with delight for what lay ahead. This could be it, the moment I had always waited for as a woman, the moment that I dreamed about, planned for, and pined for. I exercised even more care than usual while packing for our four-day adventure to Mexico.

When I went to meet Tom for the trip, I was grinning from ear to ear. I had a feeling of self-confidence and contentment. Visions of the engagement party filled my head. As we checked into the resort, I chuckled to myself, thinking that the next time we checked in somewhere could in fact be our honeymoon. As I unpacked, I envisioned all the details of how our wedding would take place.

Knowing Tom, it would be a festive occasion, one likely to draw quite a lot of attention. There could possibly be balloons, and a Mariachi band to boot, perhaps even a parasail.

Every morning, I woke with a bubbling anticipation. I took great care in getting ready each day. Usually a relatively low-maintenance girl, I took exceptional care in choosing every outfit. I spent additional time on my hair and makeup, even when going to lie out in the sun at the pool. You just never can be too sure when that special moment will strike. I wanted to look my best for the photos; I wanted to remember that special day or night forever. It was to be my Cinderella moment.

As the days wore on, I continued to daydream the sequence of events. I imagined showing complete strangers the new sparkling rock on my finger. I made special care to ensure I had a perfectly painted French manicure that would offset the new sparkly gem. I was full of mixed emotions.

Each evening as I dressed for dinner, I had the feeling I would come home engaged. Yet there was almost a bit of sadness that this moment I had waited for my entire life would be over. The feeling of being engaged was a freeing feeling, a liberating feeling. It's a feeling where you know you will never have to go on another blind date for the rest of your life. You will never again have to go through the heartbreak of being dumped. It's knowing you will never have to sit at work and have your cube mates tell you that they have the perfect guy for you and that he will be at the BBQ on Sunday, so you can meet him. It is an amazing feeling knowing you will be someone's wife and eventually someone's mother. It's a fulfilling and exhilarating feeling.

As day two and three of the vacation passed, I began to get the sinking feeling of watching the sands slip through the hourglass. I knew full well that time on this trip was running out. I began to realize by the end of the evening on the third day that I might have succumbed to the overreaction of Ash's wild imagination and idle gossip. I commanded my mind to think positively; I am a firm believer in the old adage, "You get what you focus on." It was definitely hard work to make this happen.

By the end of evening four, our last night there, my emotions had shifted dramatically. I had gone from being hopeful and full of anticipation to being full of doubt. Although I tried to keep my chin up, telling myself I must continue to believe, I knew truly, at this point, it was a losing battle.

At the end of a long dinner that was (unfortunately) free of any surprises, I decided to drown my sorrows with chocolate and order some dessert. This was truly my last-ditch effort. I thought to myself, this has to be it: he was waiting for dessert! How many times have you seen a man propose over dessert in a movie or on television? "Yes," I declared to the waiter, "I will have the chocolate lava cake." He explained to me that it would take ten minutes to make, as it was their house specialty.

"Great choice," Tom said to me. I gazed deeply into his eyes, trying to decipher exactly what he meant by that. I asked myself, did I see I glimmer, a sparkle in his eyes? Turned out later that my reading into the situation was hopeless and he really did mean that I made a great choice with the lava cake.

The wait for the cake was painful. Because it takes ten to fifteen minutes to prepare this specialty, most normal people would have seen this on the menu and ordered dessert in advance. I kept the last glimmer of hope I had alive and managed to daydream that Tom had prearranged something fancy with the chef. I just waited, hoping for the best. This seemed to be my final hope. Tom and I continued with idle chit-chat while my mind was racing a million miles a minute. I wondered how my ring would arrive: Will there be a candle in my cake with the ring around it? Will it just be delicately placed by the side of the lavish dessert? Will it come with one of those big fancy silver covers that the waiter will whisk away at the last moment before he places it in front of me, changing my life as I know it forever? Or will Tom go the riskier route? Will he have it baked directly into the dessert? Will he spoon me a delectable bite, in which I discover, after placing it in my mouth, that it contains the sparkly gem that I have been waiting for forever? The last option was a bit risky, but how romantic!

At last the waiter arrived, seeming to dump a plate of chocolate cake in front of me and then scurry off to the next table. I scratched around the chocolate with my fork like a hen pecking for worms, in hopes that during the baking process the ring had sunken to the bottom. I glanced over at Tom as he picked his teeth with a toothpick. I was disgusted. My stomach immediately dropped. No ring. At this point, the idea of stomaching even one bite of the decadent dessert seemed impossible. I didn't even want the dessert. I wished I could beam myself back home, curl up in my bed in fetal position, and pretend the whole thing never happened. I managed to scarf down a few bites of the now-hated dessert and keep a stiff upper lip, letting Tom know I was ready to go home.

When we got back to the room, I immediately knew I was facing a great deal of embarrassment. Not only was I completely devastated, but now I was going home unengaged to face my group of girlfriends. The worst part of the situation is that Ash, bless her heart, would have spread the news like wildfire in her excitement for me. This thought alone proved to be more painful and humiliating than reliving the constant horror I experienced by replaying this dinner over and over again in my head.

I woke up the next morning cheerful and bright. That is, for about the first thirty seconds, until the gloom and doom of what had happened reentered my mind. I was instantly reminded that I was going home minus one very important item than I had expected.

As I packed all my things and belongings, sulking inside, it dawned on me, if Tom didn't ask me to marry him, what did all of this mean? What does this say about the future of our relationship?

This thought proved to be more daunting and unsettling than the first. You see, at that stage of my life, I was incredibly codependent. I couldn't bear the thought, or even the possibility, of not being with this man. At that point, I had no sense of what a true identity was. I saw myself as Tom's girlfriend, never mind the humiliation of coming home from Mexico unengaged. The thought of breaking up literally gave me chest pains and made me nauseous. What would my girlfriends say when I arrived home with no ring? The inquisition would begin. In my mind it seemed like a horrible episode of Geraldo.

Due to the late-breaking development of this last incredibly stressful thought, I decided to skip being pouty all day and instead be the perfect, subservient, giving girlfriend, in hopes that this would spare me getting dumped.

Looking back, it didn't do me much good, but it made for a peaceful reentry back into the scene and back to work. Slowly but surely, I began to feel my confidence in having a future with this man shrinking. Because I couldn't cognitively bear the thought of living without him, I pretended to reassure myself that everything would be fine.

The fate-shaping moment came about a week later. It seemed to be a morning like any other. The alarm went off at approximately 6:30. I always woke up first. I nudged Tom. He was always difficult to stir in the mornings. "Honey, are you up for a roller blade?" I asked.

He sat up and exclaimed with certainty, "No!" The strangeness of his answer struck me hard, and I felt as though I had been kicked in the stomach with a fast-flying soccer ball. He followed up with, "I think we should take a break." I looked around the house; it was still overflowing with presents and decorations from the surprise party I had thrown for him only days before. I have never experienced such complete and total humiliation before. I made a decision at that instant that would change my life forever. Forget that fact that I had given him three great years of my life. Forget the fact that I had catered to him, spoiled him, cherished him, and been faithful to him. In that moment, I decided not to fight, sensing that God had a plan for me that was bigger than what I could see right then. It was if everything in my being was leading me toward my real destiny. Although the pain seemed almost unbearable, I knew I would be taken care of, and that it would all make sense one day.

I spent the next few hours gathering all of my belongings from the last three years. I choked back the tears as I made trip after trip out to my SUV, filling it with memories and dreams lost.

That next year proved to be one of the most difficult in my life up to that point. I felt pain, loss, and sadness that I had never before imagined possible. I cried my eyes out day and night. I lost fifteen pounds almost immediately on what my girlfriends and I have coined "the break-up diet." I could hardly make myself eat. At night I couldn't sleep, and if I did, I had daunting dreams. In the early morning hours, I would run up the steep San Francisco hills for a workout, powered solely on adrenaline and anxiety. I was only able to eat a quarter of a bagel each morning and coffee throughout the day. There became an unspoken rule at our house that I lived in that we weren't to watch any television or movies that had any sort of a love story in them. I ripped up journal entries and pictures and destroyed helpless stuffed animals. I was angry, I was hurt, and I was destroyed. Or so I thought. The reality of the situation is that I was experiencing one of the most amazing gifts I had ever received. I was learning!

This truly was a period of overwhelming sadness for me. It was also the ignition that propelled me on to a path of self-growth like no other. It is my belief today that every relationship and break-up you experience is part of a larger process to prepare you for lessons you need to know. Relationships can serve as a magnifying glass to show you what is working and what is not working in your life. If used correctly, relationships can be an excellent tool to allow you to attract whatever it is you desire in your life.

Immediately after this breakup, I began to feel a sense of relief. I started to feel like myself again. I no longer felt like someone who lived her life for others, but I felt like someone who mattered and had a purpose. It was freeing, liberating. I felt a new hope and relief that one day I would truly be happy and loved for who I was.

During my relationship with Tom, I thought I had been truly happy. I thought that I knew who I was and what I wanted and that I had everything I had ever dreamed of. The truth was that I had no idea what I really wanted and no idea of who I really was. It terrifies me to think what my life would be like today if things had gone the way I wanted, if I was still in that relationship, married to

Tom. Although the heartbreak I experienced was painful, it was necessary to guide me to where I am today and toward true happiness.

I have learned so many lessons from relationships that didn't last. One of the more powerful lessons I have learned is that you can't count on other people to make you happy. It is not possible. You must find happiness within yourself to experience a full life and to be able to share your life with others. I have also learned that you must meet your own needs. During my relationship with Tom, I depended on him for happiness and fulfillment; this in itself was a major contributor to the tremendous heartbreak and pain I experienced once that relationship ended. I had such an intense, all-encompassing desire to be loved that I overlooked many of the extenuating circumstances in the relationship that hindered long-term success. If I had stayed with Tom, I would have ended up very lonely and miserable. I would have, in essence, become a single mom and had more than my share of the weight on my shoulders. But at the time I was unable to identify what qualities I needed in a relationship. I had chosen someone who was a workaholic, who didn't place a great deal of importance on our relationship. I had not yet learned that there is someone out there who would love me for who I am.

It is more important for a woman to be happy alongside her man than to make her man happy. I constantly coach clients who are focused on making their men happy, and they don't realize that what would make their men happy is if they are happy themselves. Being happy can be such an easy thing to do, but it is generally overlooked.

There are many reasons we enter into and stay in relationships that don't work. Going through the break up of relationships can become frustrating, especially if your ultimate goal is to meet someone, marry him, and plan your future together. The key is to become an expert in learning from relationships. Be incredibly honest with yourself on the choices you have made and what the communication breakdowns were.

From the research I have done, including many, many teary nights with girlfriends on couches, with a bottle of wine and a box of Kleenex, I have identified some patterns on why women enter into relationships that don't work.

The first reason women enter into relationships that don't work is that we tend to blindly enter into relationships with people who have a past that we would not necessarily approve of. This can show up in many different ways. It can be a simple habit, such as too many nights out drinking with the boys, or as complex as a pattern of cheating on ex-girlfriends. So many times we try to convince ourselves that this time it will be different. We will be the one to change this behavior. It always fails! Always! Don't get me wrong: I am a huge believer in our ability to change and grow. I have observed too many painful breakups that are a result of ignoring negative behavior that existed in the first place. It is unrealistic to believe that if you choose a partner who drinks a lot and goes out to clubs dancing, this behavior will change once you are in love. The same goes for someone who cheats on his partner to enter a relationship with you.

Most people tend to repeat the patterns that they have experienced in previous relationships. There are two lessons you can learn from these past patterns; both are equally valuable. The first lesson is to steer clear of men who behave in ways that are unacceptable to you. The second lesson is to understand what is lacking in your life and, once understood, to fulfill that need yourself.

Ignoring red flags is another huge warning sign that I have observed in various deteriorating relationships. We have those nagging voices in our heads, hearts, and guts, but we ignore them for whatever reason. Usually it is because we are entranced with some sort of fantasy that tells us this time it will be different. My belief is that we are all guided by some sort of higher power and that our soul tells us which choices we should make. This is not to say that we will always make the correct choices. This is also not to say that all choices, even the bad ones, will not lead to some level of happiness rather than pain. Choices that lead to pain can most times lead to a greater happiness once that lesson has been learned. I do believe, however, that at some level we always know what the correct choices are. This knowledge can show up differently for each person. Sometimes it is a guiding voice inside your head, almost as if to say, "Don't do it." For others it can be a tug on the heart to inform you that you are making an incorrect decision. For others still, it can be a sinking feeling in your gut that shows up every time your decisions aren't made with absolute truth. However this shows up for you, it is critical that you listen. By heeding these warnings you can guide yourself into what is truthful and real for you.

Another reason women don't have successful relationships is because there is no clear distinction between romantic love and friendship love. Sometimes we can find ourselves in relationships where the person seems as if they are our best buddy. We love to spend time with them and care for them deeply, but there is some component that is missing that prevents us from being deeply in love with them.

I had an experience once where I was in a relationship where everything went smoothly. There was a deep caring, but a lack of sexual intimacy. I did everything in my power to convince myself that things were fine. I would tell myself that this sexual intimacy wasn't important and that you are always hearing that once people get married it goes away or as you get older it really becomes less and less important. It wasn't until two things happened that I realized how ridiculous this was. First, the relationship ended and I realized in my truth that an intimate connection is crucial for me. Second, I was later able to experience a relationship with an incredible sexual connection and passion that was healthy. I didn't realize that aside from the pleasure and gratification that comes from an intimate relationship, it also serves to create a depth of bonding that can't be replicated. This is just one example that I have experienced personally, and there are dozens of others that have equally as profound effects.

The fear of being alone is another huge factor I have seen in relationships that do not last. It has been my experience that so many people choose to stay in a relationship for fear that they won't be able to find something better or that what they want doesn't exist. This can be a very lonely place to be. It is my belief that there is absolutely someone for everyone. I used to believe that there is just one person out there for everyone. I formed this belief because my parents were high school sweethearts and had been together since they were fifteen and sixteen years old. I went around for twenty-three years of my life always searching for the perfect soul mate, hoping that by some twist of fate, I would encounter that chance meeting that would change my life forever. This belief shifted when my mother passed away when I was twenty-three years old. If it were true that there was only one person for everyone, this meant my father would be alone for the rest of his life with no chance of happiness or finding someone to fall in love with. The truth is that my father did, in time, fall in love again and remarry, and he is very happy. I had to reformulate my belief to "there is someone for everyone at every stage of the life."

The other thing that I learned is that you can be with the one that you are meant to be with right now, but that person might not be the one for you forever. I call this person "Mr. Right Now." He is in your life to teach you a lesson, and by learning that lesson, you will in turn be on your path to meeting "Mr. Right." I believe through all of my research that there are many people who come into our lives to teach us valuable lessons. These lessons may deal with life, or love, or faith. It may be that this person is meant to be around for a short period of time but that the lessons will last forever.

Another failing formula is to get caught up in the promise of a fairytale future. It is sometimes easy to get caught up in the idea of what something will be like one day, rather than what it already is now. It becomes very easy to lose sight of what is going on now when someone is constantly promising you how things will be in the future. When you are in a relationship like this, it is easy to sacrifice what is truly important to you. My experience has been that the payoff never seems to come. Most times, the relationship remains the way it currently is. A good indicator of the future of a relationship is the current state of a relationship. There will always be times in life when things are busy and needs aren't being met short-term, for whatever reason, but this is not a good place to stay long-term. I remember being in a relationship with a workaholic where I was constantly being promised that the reasons he was working so hard and didn't have time to spend with me was because he wanted us to have a strong financial future together. For years, I put up with this and prevented myself from being in a relationship that met my needs. Eventually I tired of showing up for weddings alone and countless nights of take-out food on the couch while he was working late or away on a business trip. Eventually the relationship ended. Now, five years later, when I speak to him on the phone, nothing has changed in that area. He is still working around the clock with what I would call little semblance of a quality of life or relationship. When he speaks of his relationships, he tells me that his girlfriend is always nagging him because he doesn't spend enough time with her and he is always at work.

These are just some of the many lessons that can be learned from relationships that don't necessarily last. As I said before, make yourself an expert on learning why relationships you have had in the past didn't work out, and it will serve as a treasure map toward your future successful relationship. Once you get this area down pat and become your own true soul mate, you can't help but attract everything you desire into your life.

5

Loving Yourself First

Self-love leads to true love.

I believe there are two types of people in this world: those who look before they leap and those who leap before they look. I definitely fall into the latter category. "Leaping before looking" can create results in one of two ways. On the one hand, it can prove you to be courageous and brave. On the other hand, it can cause you to get in a bit over your head at times.

A few years back, while I was pursuing one of my dreams of becoming a holistic health practitioner and attending school full time, I got the bright idea of becoming a yoga instructor to supplement my income. I scoured the Internet to see what I could find as far as teacher training courses for yoga instructors.

Perfect! That didn't take long, I thought to myself. I found a program that looked amazing. The Web site featured a picture of a beautiful woman doing a balance pose on a turquoise deck overlooking the crashing sea. Reading further, I learned that the yoga retreat was on the sunny island of Nassau, in the Bahamas. Sign me up! I quickly scrolled down to learn the price. Much to my surprise, it was actually affordable, $1600. I won't have to teach that many classes to get a return on my investment, I thought to myself. I grabbed my credit card and entered all of my important details. Looking back, there was also a great deal of other pertinent information regarding the course on the Web site. Honestly, I couldn't be bothered reading all of that. I was going to the Bahamas to become a yoga instructor. I had girlfriends I needed to brag to, cute yoga outfits to buy.

I picked up the phone and began to dial numbers madly of all of the girlfriends I could reach to share this exciting news. I immediately reached my friend Sherry, who was extremely excited for me. In my excitement, I managed to convince her into attending with me.

As the course approached, I began to feel my excitement and anticipation growing. We arrived at the ashram late into the evening before the first day of class. A large storm had moved through the island. After three flights and a shuttle ride to get there, check-in couldn't have come soon enough for me.

My boyfriend at the time had the smarts to print out the "What to do when you arrive" portion of the Web site. I dug into my purse to find the instructions. It instructed us to call the ashram water taxi to come pick us up. I fumbled again through my purse to locate a quarter and dropped it into the pay phone. I dialed the number and someone on the other end answered in Sanskrit. I found this to be a bit peculiar, but just chalked it up to some overzealous student showing off their yoga learnings. I let the fleeting thought go, as I was anxious to get out of the rain and get settled.

The boat arrived shortly after the call, and we had a brisk ten-minute ride on the choppy waters in the pouring rain. Upon arrival, we schlepped all of our tents and gear to the registration area. They let us know that due to heavy rains they were going to put us up in a cabin for the night, and we could set up out tents at daybreak.

Morning came and we set up our tents and toured around the property. The air was moist and foggy; there was a dewy smell in the air. The energy on the property was amazing. I could almost feel a spiritual presence around me. There was Indian music playing faintly in the background and I could overhear the regular residents exchanging their morning pleasantries. We met a few of the other students and learned that we were to meet in the temple that evening for opening night. So far, so good. I was full of anticipation and excitement and visualized myself back home in San Diego teaching my yoga classes. I thought to myself, these thirty days will be great; I will get in tremendously great shape, tanned, toned, and relaxed.

Evening came soon enough and we were off to the temple for opening night. That evening I pretty much scared myself straight. We entered the temple at six o'clock to find multiple swamis dressed in orange robes and chanting Sanskrit songs, one after the other. One swami would bang on the tambourine while another played the sitar. This went on for an hour and a half straight before anyone spoke a word. I became increasingly nervous and questioned myself as to why I had signed up for this.

When I was a young girl, my grandmother used to say, "When in Rome, do as the Romans do." Although hearing this as a young girl used to irritate me profusely, I decided I had no other option than to succumb, and I began to hum along with the music. I absolutely drew the line on banging any type of tambourine or other homemade musical instrument. I sat for hours on the cold, hard, cement floor of the temple in meditation pose. The students passed around a basket of musical instruments as well as lyric sheets. The swamis continued chanting and strumming their sitars and accordion-like instruments.

Surely, I thought to myself, this had to be some sort of special deal for opening night. This program can't be this strange. It is impossible. Could it be? The chanting eventually subsided and the head swami began to speak—in Sanskrit. The evening wore on for hours. My mind toggled back and forth from paying some sort of attention to trying to conjure up an excuse as to why I had to leave the island immediately and return home. I visualized myself at the airport jumping on the next flight. I would focus in for a moment on what they were saying; I couldn't help wondering to myself when they would be handing out Kool-Aid.

A few hours had passed and I found myself bowing down on my knees in front of a beautiful altar that featured a shrine of Buddha and many other deities. Then, bowing again after my name had been called in front of the head swami, I received a red dot on my forehead; this dot was not to be removed. The swami began to whisper some sort of Sanskrit in my ear.

Upon returning to my tent and reflecting on my peculiar day, I deduced that I was in way over my head. I had learned that we would be practicing yoga and the yogi principles for sixteen hours each day, for the next thirty days. There would be no contact with the outside world, except for three pay phones shared between 250 people and a board where e-mails sent to us would be posted each day. We would learn the four yamas of yoga and eat, sleep, and breathe them. There were to be no mirrors, no make-up, no hair dryers, and, heck, no electricity for that matter. Only five-minute showers. Sleeping outside in a tent. No jewelry. Ridiculous uniforms that were to be kept clean at all times. (This in itself would prove to be a daunting task, as we were outdoors, and the uniform consisted of a pair of white pants and a light yellow shirt.) No alcohol, no caffeine. Vegan meals served twice a day. The good news is that we would have five hours free each Friday; otherwise, we were tasked every minute of every day.

I found myself confused. Part of me was frustrated and angry. The other part, which is always up for a challenge, was intrigued. I resolved to be excited about the opportunity and decided to give it my all. Weeks went by with no contact with the outside world.

The daily schedule proved to be grueling. Up at 5:30 each day, showered and in the temple by 6:00 for meditation and prayer. The rest of the day was filled with morning readings from the Bhagavad-Gita Gita, the Vedanta Bible, morning yoga asana class, breakfast, philosophy class, study hour, theoretical studies of the Bhagavad-Gita Gita, afternoon philosophy class, afternoon yoga asana class, dinner and chores, meditation and chanting, symposium lecture. Day in and day out, week in and week out, the same schedule.

Now remember, I am someone who has a passion for self-growth. This was not my first experience in a self-growth situation. I had read hundreds of books, listened to countless tape programs, and attended hundreds of hours of seminars. My challenge had been to not become overwhelmed with each and every theory or person I studied. At home, I would do my morning meditation each day that I learned from one specific guru. I would do my Hour of Power that I learned from another. I would do Oprah's daily morning questions and incantations. It sometimes seemed as though I had little time for anything else.

I was enthralled with everything that I was learning, yet a tad fearful that this experience would add to the list of daily rituals that I needed to practice in my life in order to manifest the life of my dreams. It would be another item on the list of mantras and activities that vowed to help me create all the love, peace, and happiness that I wanted in my life. And then it hit me. I was in about my third week of yoga hell. I was sitting in meditation pose in my daily philosophy class. I was half paying attention to the swami and half trying to shift my body so I could work out some type of comfortable way to sit day in and day out in meditation pose on the cold, hard floors of the temple.

I finally couldn't tolerate the torture any more. I got up and stormed out of the temple. I ran for a few minutes and then dropped down to sit on a tree stump in front of one of the cabins. I had my head draped over my arms as tears steamed down my face. I was frustrated, I was tired, and I was exhausted. At that moment I heard Swami Antiananda say my name. He said that I shouldn't cry and that the tears were unnecessary. I explained that I had had enough. I came here because I wanted to be a yoga instructor and that I didn't want to do all of this other stuff anymore. He looked at me, deep into my eyes, and said you must love yourself to truly be free. Free of all attachments and free to experience life and love. As he walked away, I half shrugged off his words; they were always stating some kind of positive mantras.

Not wanting to be a quitter, I snuck back into the temple and repositioned myself on my meditation cushion. The swami was speaking about loving yourself first. And that is when it hit me. It was as if multiple synapses in my brain were coming together at one time, creating a fireworks show of Fourth of July proportions. I finally understood one of the finer secrets of life. I had been hearing it and reading it the entire time, but for some reason, in this setting it finally sunk in. It had to be one of the greatest secrets in life. The key to attracting the love that you want in your life is to love yourself first. Not just to say it, but to mean it, to feel it, to actually and truly sincerely love yourself. The concept was so simple, yet so profound at the same time. The greatest part is that this is also the secret to attracting anything else you desire in your life. It starts with you first. It was also in that moment; one of the most important moments in my life, that I realized everyone had been saying the same thing. From Gandhi to Buddha, Anthony Robbins to Zig Ziglar. My mother, aunts, grandmother, and practically every book I had ever read on self-growth had said it. It was such an incredibly freeing feeling. It wasn't that I needed to do more in my life; I needed to integrate everything I had learned and give myself the gift of loving myself, so I could then in turn love others.

One of the ancient forms of yoga we studied was called the first Brahmavihara. This is an ancient practice of Buddhism. Its principle is to cultivate the Sanskrit word *metta,* which means "love" or "loving kindness," into our lives. The true definition of *metta* is kind, unconditional well-wishing. It is an open-hearted nurturing of ourselves and others: accepting ourselves and others just as we (and they) are, rather than for how we would want them to be. There are many different ways to create this love and teach yourself this love and kindness.

In the Buddhist practice, *metta* is learned through incanting phrases over and over again to yourself, creating somewhat of a mantra. Some examples of what you could create for a mantra include the following: "May I have love," "May I be free," "May I have joy," "May I have health," and so on. This is extremely powerful when integrated into any type of meditation of yoga practice, and is also extremely helpful when used in your everyday life. For example, you can practice chanting while you are running on the treadmill at the gym, standing in line at the supermarket or at the bank, out for a run, driving the kids to soccer or ballet. You get the point. The important thing is to use it and to live it. It will help you manifest anything that you desire into your life, especially when you go around chanting, "Bring me my soul mate." (OK, perhaps that might actually scare them away.) What would be great to focus on are the characteristics you desire in your relationships. If you want a man, or friendships that are healthy, wealthy and wise, chant that. I truly believe you get what you focus on and if you are intending that you will get a man, you will.

The more you learn to love yourself and the more that your actions come out of loving kindness, the more you will attract the love you desire into your life. If you chose to integrate this practice into your journey, I recommend spending at least twenty minutes a day with your loving mantra.

The second practice to help you start loving yourself is to listen to your inner monologue. Many of us are unaware that thousands of times day we are being self-critical. This may manifest itself in our blatant insecurities. It can also show up as our inner dialogue that is running all of the time. Try this little experiment: Find a stopwatch and set the timer for one minute. Sit still somewhere with your eyes closed and try not to have any thoughts at all cross your mind. Did you try it? If so, my guess is that it was difficult for you to make it even ten seconds without some sort of self-judgment or self-critical statement. It may have shown up in the form of "Am I doing this right?" or "I am awful at this, I can't do it, I always fail at things like this." Regardless of how it showed up for you, the lesson is a powerful one.

As women, we are constantly comparing ourselves to other women. We are criticizing ourselves and critiquing ourselves based on other people we see and based on magazines and television. Whether it is about our bodies, or abilities, or our feelings of inadequacy, we are reinforcing these beliefs by repeating them over and over again internally, sometimes even without realizing it. Can you imagine what this does to our psychology and to what we attract into our lives?

There is an old adage that states, "You get what you give." Once you begin to focus on your internal dialogue and your opinion of your self-worth, it begins to become clear how we could have attracted some of the negative, failed relationships in the past, with this entire negative racket going on.

True growth and movement into loving yourself occurs when you are able to shift this inner monologue. It is important to create new, positive mantras to replace the old negative sayings. This is where metta comes into practice. You can take these theories and principles and simply apply them to the negative dialogue you experience. When you find yourself self-criticizing, replace the critical dialogue with one of the metta statements. For example, if you are in a class at the gym and you notice a woman that possesses a quality you would like to have, stop asking yourself, "Why does she have such a great body?" or "Why am I so out of shape?" or "Why do men always go for women that look like that?" Instead, replace this dialogue with "May I have love," or "May I have health," or "May I have happiness." This step may sound incredibly simple, but at the same time, it is incredibly profound in your growth toward self-love. I guarantee you, if you do this one thing, you will be amazed at the rewards you reap from it and the transformations you will have. It will not only change your ability to love yourself and others, it will also give you the confidence and power to go after the other things you desire in life.

The third exercise in learning to love yourself is to consciously take some time to recognize and celebrate everything you truly love about yourself. I know this sounds simple, but it is rare that we take the time to acknowledge ourselves and celebrate what is wonderful about ourselves. This is a fun activity. I am going to take you back to the basics and bring back the days of finger painting, glue sticks, and glitter. Your assignment is to create a "Poster of Love." Here's how:

1. I recommend getting a poster board or a large fun-colored paper. On the top, write out "I love..." Fill the entire board with everything that is truly wonderful about yourself and your life. This is just for you. You may chose to share it, or you may use it as a powerful reminder of what an amazing person you are, a person deserving of love. Regardless, you must go all-out while creating the poster.

2. I also recommend carving out some space on your poster to write out all the different qualities you love about yourself. Create another section of your poster that includes all of the qualities you would like to manifest into your life. This is your intention section. (We will be doing some additional exercises with this later on.)

3. Once this intention section is completed, state your intentions out loud every day. For example, if your intention list includes laughter and forgiveness, state your manifesting this into your life out loud. To do this, sit in a quiet, private area, facing your poster. State out loud, "I intend to have a life full of laughter. I intend to have a life full of forgiveness." The simple act of writing these down and stating them out loud each day will ensure that your mind is focused on attracting them into your life whenever possible.

4. Another great idea for your poster is to take pictures of yourself doing the things that you love. If your family and friends are your most important values, then take some pictures of happy moment with your friends and family. If you love the fact that you are nurturing, take a picture of yourself caring for a small child or sibling. Make a collage on your poster with these pictures as a visual celebration and reminder of what you already love about yourself. Yet another idea is to include ribbons or medals from events you are proud of.

When your poster is complete, celebrate it. Celebrate each and every one of the qualities you love about yourself. Celebrating can include any type of ritual you desire. You can play your favorite song and dance around wildly, have a special cocktail, or break out in contagious laughter, whatever you desire. The final part of celebrating includes stating out loud everything you already love about yourself. Put on your favorite tune and state out loud, "I love my compassion. I love my ability to be a great listener." Celebrate whatever is on your poster.

The last activity in this chapter deals with admiring. Admiring is a concept that, simply put, has you take someone or something that you would like to have or be like, and then try to create in your own life what they do or have. For this exercise, I want you to model the love you are currently giving to others in your life. If you are anything like me and the hundreds of other women I know, you are probably quickly discounting the love that you already have in your life and your ability to be a great lover. It is infinitely easier to love others than it is to love ourselves. Whether this is love toward a past significant other, siblings, friends, or grandparents, it is always much easier to love someone else than it is to show love toward ourselves. Learning to love ourselves is a skill, and just like any other skill, it takes practice. Luckily, it is something that can easily be learned. It is just a matter of discovering the recipe and repeating it over and over again.

For this process, it is necessary for you to make a list of the top five people who you love in your life. Again, this love can be for anyone, even the family dog. The important thing is not who you love, but rather that you create the list. Once you have created this list, you will need five additional pieces of binder paper. Write out one of the five names on the top of each piece of paper. One by one, on each piece of paper, write out all of the ways that you express your love to each of these people. Write what you love about them, how that makes you feel, and how you share your love with them. This is an extremely important part of the exercise. Highlight on each of the five pages your strategy for showing these people your love. It can be as simple of giving them a compliment or a flower or writing them a note expressing your gratitude for them in your life. It can be a hug, or a look that only you two share, with a knowing that you love each other. There are no right or wrong answers here. The key is to create an understanding and a recipe of how you show your love to others. Once you have completed this part of the exercise, you have your recipe for showing love. Spend some time reading over your recipe and create a separate page on how you will now implement those strategies into loving yourself and showing yourself the same loving kindness that you show others. I guarantee you, once you put this recipe into practice and truly begin to love yourself, it will just be a matter of time before you attract all of your deepest desires into your life.

I know I have thrown a lot at you this chapter. This is because I believe that loving yourself is absolutely the most important thing you can to do attract love into your life. Above that, it is the single most important thing you can do to create a life full of happiness and abundance in all areas of your life. Be gentle and kind to yourself through these exercises. You have been living your life a certain way up until now, and you are realizing some profound things about yourself. All of these exercises take practice. It is unrealistic to think that you can just read one chapter and spend a few hours doing some exercises, and then all of a sudden, things will be different. It takes repetition. Lots of it. If you find you are working on your metta and you are still conjuring up some negative feelings, be gentle. Sometimes in life, when you feel that something is not working, that is the time when it actually *is* working. It is just like going to the gym. You don't go to the gym one time and all of the sudden expect to have perfectly toned muscles. It takes continuous practice and repetition. As you continue your workouts, it becomes much easier, and working out becomes a habit. You begin to become fit. The same thing will happen with your emotions. Celebrate your successes, honor your poster, and give yourself the gift of love that you are already giving others.

6

The List

It is absolutely critical to know exactly what you are looking for in order to find it.

The other day, I was in desperate need of a new black suit. I travel all of the time for my job and am frequently at events where I have to look very professional. So there I was, thumbing through the racks at some boutiques in one of my favorite towns. Suddenly, what appeared to be the perfect suit jumped out at me. At first glance it looked amazing. It was black, tailored, and one of my favorite labels. I got very excited of the prospect of having found exactly what I was looking for. Or so I thought. I rushed to the dressing room full of anticipation and high hopes.

I put the jacket on first. It was a perfect fit. The way it was tailored was extremely flattering and made me look very sharp. Then something happened. While I was celebrating the fact that I would have to look no further, I got a glimpse of the suit in a different light. I thought to myself, "Is this suit black or charcoal?" As I glanced in the mirror, I was able to convince myself that the suit was black, which was what I was looking for. Then it came time to try on the pants. This is where things went drastically wrong. They could not have fit worse. They were way too baggy, and it was hard to believe that they were supposed to go with this amazingly tailored jacket. I tried to convince myself that I could have them taken in. I even believed it for a while. Then I looked at myself deep in the mirror and had a realization. Why would I settle for something that isn't perfect, just because it looked like it was the right thing in the beginning? Then I realized this is a huge metaphor for life. Where else in my life was I trying to convince myself something was black, when it was clearly charcoal, just to avoid the agony of having to keep looking? I realized that this is all too common when we are making big decisions in life, such as our relationships and our careers. I vowed never to take the easy route and to always keep looking for what it is I truly desire in life, even if it meant battling traffic and the crowds at the mall. I deserved the best. We all do!

This is where the concept of the list comes in. Whatever it is you are going after in life: a suit, a job, a boyfriend, a husband, it is critical that you know exactly what you are looking for. Otherwise, you have no chance of finding it. Once you have that clarity, never settle for less. Be specific and concise and make sure you only accept that. Here is how you comprise your own list. Take a simple piece of binder paper and write at the top "My Dream Life." I recommend creating a sacred place to do this exercise. Create a place that is free from distractions of the modern world and free from any negative energy. You may want to light some candles or incense or essential oils. Put one of your favorite CDs into the player. Choose one that you find to be both inspiring and romantic. Once you are settled and have ten minutes to spare, begin to write madly all that you desire in your life. There are no restrictions or boundaries. Nothing is too small or too big to include on your list. It may be difficult at first. If nothing comes to mind, try to envision a few of the relationships that you admire, and write down some of those characteristics. Envision your perfect job, your ideal living space, your ideal body. Once you start to fill the page, ideas will flow. Anything at all that you feel may be an important quality or attribute or item to have, jot down on your list. Imagine that you have a catalog with endless possibilities, and it is your job to order the perfect life for yourself. You are able to order anything you want, but once you have ordered you are stuck with it, so make sure to order carefully. Include everything that you would possibly need, want, and desire to live your dream life.

There are also some very important areas to hit on when creating your list. I call these your VIP areas. VIP stands for values, interests, and principles. The first part to focus on is values. It is crucial that when you are defining your desires that your values are aligned in order to achieve long-term success.

The second area you want to focus on when creating your list is interests. It is also important to make sure that you are nurturing yourself with all of your interests. Ask yourself if there is anything you have always wanted to do but never made the time for. What types of activities do you find interesting? What types of activities do you admire that you have seen others perform?

The last portion of the list you will want to focus on is principles. It is important to define exactly what you will and will not tolerate in your life. Again, just as with the interests, be as specific as possible. Write out all of the things that you will stand for and things that you won't stand for.

The key is to only make decisions and take action in the direction that is consistent with your list. For each decision you make, ask yourself if it is in line with your dream life.

Once you have your list, you are well on your way. My belief is that the clarity of what you are looking for is the most important component in long-term happiness and fulfillment. Absolute and total clarity on what you are looking for. This is not to say that as you learn and grow your list can't change over time. Through your experiences in life you may chose to add or delete certain components of your list. It is a process, a tool. The list will act as your guide in selecting activities, interests, and relationships that are supportive to you.

I will offer just one caveat with your list. Be flexible. Sometimes the best gifts in life come in an unexpected package. Do not ever compromise on the important aspects of your list, such as values; instead, be open to the idea that what you are looking for may show up in many different ways.

Once you have created your list, honor it. One thing I and many of my girlfriends, as well as women I have coached, have found helpful is to do intentions with your list. There are many different ways to do intentions. They can be done in a group or by yourself, whichever way you are most comfortable. It can be as easy as reading your list out loud each day starting with "I intend to attract _____ into my life." Repeat these intentions until you have gone entirely through your list. The power of focus alone will ensure that you are attracting these traits into your life. Another thing that many women have found powerful is to keep their list with them at all times. Sleep with it under your pillow. This alone will help to manifest it into your life. You can also create a smaller version of your list that you can place on your desk at work or in your daily planner.

I cannot stress enough how critical the list is. Living without a list it is almost like trying to navigate to an unknown destination without a map. I guarantee you, once you have clarity on what it is you are looking for and you are focused on it, it is just a matter of time before you find it.

7

Knowing When to Let Go

Knowing when to move on can be just as important as knowing what you are looking for.

It suddenly dawned on me after about six weeks of dating Anthony that I hadn't been to Whole Foods the entire time we were together. This seemed very odd to me, because it was my favorite place to shop and eat. I had also started a small business on the side where I taught nutritional coaching and created cleansing and detoxification packages for people, which led to Whole Foods being my second home.

This is actually how I bonded with Anthony. I had just gotten out of an eighteen-month relationship and was feeling pretty bummed about it. My friend Jolene had told me about some yoga meditation and chanting at a yoga studio a half hour away. I was not yet ready to do any serious socializing, but I agreed to go because I know how powerful yoga can be for healing. The evening was magnificent. I realized I was holding on to a great deal of sadness and guilt from my previous relationship, and I was able to process some of my emotions and let them go. After the experience, Jolene asked me if I would accompany her to a local restaurant and bar to meet a friend of hers who was having a birthday. I refused, explaining that I was tired and that I wasn't dressed properly. She pleaded with me, letting me know she didn't want to go alone and that it would be fun. We made a quick stop by her house, and Jolene dressed me in some of her fun "going out" attire. When we arrived at the bar, I felt a bit uncomfortable. I still was not yet ready to date. Almost immediately I ran into one of my guy friends from college that I had not seen in a very long time. He was gorgeous. We hit it off. We ended up spending the evening reminiscing about the good old days. I gave him and a friend of his a ride home, and we exchanged numbers. He called me the next day. Even though I had vowed to only date people who shared the values I had written in my list, I mistakenly made a few exceptions—he seemed like a lot of fun.

A few days into the relationship, he learned about my new business and was extremely interested. I justified his interest in what I was doing as an interest in holistic healing, thus making it easier for me to ignore some of the blatant qualities that contradicted my list. I was looking for was someone who wasn't into partying and who rarely drank alcohol. Anthony became increasingly interested in my cleansing programs. Within a week or so I had Anthony two of his brothers, and many of his coworkers on a cleanse. His interest allowed me to feel as though we had one of my passions in common. It also provided us a great deal of quality time, free from socializing out at the bars, to get to know each other. What I didn't realize then was that Anthony spent most of his time partying with friends and coworkers and taking clients out for steak dinners. This couldn't have been more opposite to what I was actually looking for and what I had written on my relationship list. As time went by I began to like him more and more, which made it easier for me to overlook the list and what was truly important to me. I justified his faults, telling myself that it was important to be open to different types of people. This was fine for a month or so until I realized that I was changing my behavior to accommodate what was important to him, not to me. I found myself going out for drinks with him and his friends, something I had not done for four years. I spent less time working out and working on my business and more time trying to impress Anthony.

It suddenly dawned on me six weeks into the relationship, as I pulled into the Whole Foods parking lot, that I hadn't been there since I met Anthony. I knew that something was up and that I needed to make some changes.

It is easy to find yourself in these types of situations where you don't have exactly what it is you desire, whether it is with a job, a friendship, or an intimate relationship. Of course, when you do find yourself in this specific situation, I believe a higher power intervenes and takes action before you get a chance to. This chapter covers the importance of relationships. The relationships in your life can be a direct reflection of how you feel about yourself and what you think you deserve.

I was walking down the aisle in Whole Foods when my phone rang. It was Anthony. He was canceling our date that evening and instead going to drink beer at the baseball game with his brothers. He said he would call me later, but he didn't. It didn't matter to me. I vowed to make it a date night with myself. I purchased an extravagant dinner and had an evening filled with candles, a wonderful dinner, and a bubble bath. A few days after this, while we were having lunch and some margaritas at a local Mexican joint, he broke up with me completely out of the blue. I was shocked and sad. I enjoyed hanging out with him. It was somewhat of a painful breakup for me, given the fact that we only spent a very short time together. Looking back, I realize it was more painful because I knew deep down that I had compromised what was important to me just to have a relationship. When I had finally come to my senses, I decided to get out my list and identify what traits Anthony and I really did have in common. That made me realize that I had been with the wrong person and that I needed to keep looking.

There are so many reasons people stay in relationships with the wrong partners. When I coach I am always amazed at how many people in unhealthy relationships have the mistaken belief that things will get better or that their current situation is good enough. When I ask them directly if this is their ideal mate, they tell me no. If you are currently in a relationship or in a job that is not meeting your needs, it not only causes you grief and pain in the short-term, it can actually prevent you from finding what you truly desire in the long-term.

Below I've listed some of the common reasons women choose to stay in the wrong relationships or careers. All of them should be avoided, but if you find one or more of these sounding familiar, it is not too late to make the necessary changes.

- *Fear of having made the wrong choice.* As I explained in the story about Anthony, I knew that I had made the wrong choice. I didn't want to admit this to myself because I felt as though I should have known better. Looking back on the situation, my girlfriends' reactions when I told them we were dating should have raised a huge red flag. All of them were surprised and said that they didn't really see us together. At that point of my life and newly out of a serious relationship, I really wanted to have found a new relationship. I overlooked all of this for a short time and told myself that they were wrong. I should have just listened to them in the first place. I could have avoided a lot of pain from the breakup and been that much closer to finding Mr. Right.

- *Fear of failure.* So many times, we are too scared to admit that we might have wasted all of our time and energy in something that does not work. This can be a frustrating realization. Once you realize that you are in a relationship or a job that does not have long-term potential, the best thing you can do is get out of it as soon as you can. All staying does is prolong the inevitable and keep you from being free, available, and healthy for the right relationship and career.

- *Fear of hurting the other person.* We think that if we stay with Mr. Wrong we are doing him more good than harm. The truth is that deep down everyone knows when something is not right. There are many ways that you might deny this fact and try to perceive that everything is fine, but it is just a matter of time before the truth will be discovered. This is why people will sometimes have affairs to get out of a relationship. I have coached clients who actually believed they wanted to get caught cheating on their girlfriends. They believed that this would allow them to get out of their relationship without hurting the other person. The truth is that such deception causes much more pain than being honest with the person and letting him or her know your true feelings. Honesty is always the best policy. The sooner you allow the other person to heal and move on, the sooner you both will be able to find your perfect partner.

- *Fear that there really isn't someone out there for you.* This simply isn't true. Depending on what your belief system is, this fear can cause you not to put yourself in a position where you can find the perfect partner. I have said it before and I will say it again: I believe that there is someone out there for everyone at every stage of her life. The more you learn and change and grow, the more you have a chance of meeting the right person for you. Many times women are scared to leave a relationship because they believe it will be a long time before they find another one. What often happens is that, if the necessary lessons are learned from the current relationship, a new, healthy, successful one can be found very soon. I have seen so many women find new partners shortly after leaving a dead-end relationship. If you look at each relationship you have like a stepping-stone to the next, this concept makes a lot of sense. As long as you are genuinely learning the lessons you need to learn and not repeating the same patterns, it is logical that the next relationship you have will be more successful.

I know this chapter is different from the others. It might even be painful if you identify with these circumstances in your own relationship. I felt relationships are a necessary topic to cover because it can often be the stumbling block that prevents people from entering into the right relationship for them. This can be a relationship in your career, family, or personal life. As with everything in your life, if you are honest with yourself and with your partner, everything else will take care of itself.

8

Girlfriends

.

Having a support network that you can trust, depend on, share with, and confide in is invaluable.

It is a challenge for me to condense all of the stories on this topic into one chapter. I believe that having a group of girlfriends you can share your life experiences with is one of the single most important things you can do for a happy, healthy life. I am happy to share some of my stories with you in hopes that you realize the importance of girlfriends in your own lives and honor, nurture, and strengthen your existing relationships. I want to share as many specific examples with you as I can to reiterate the importance of this subject.

About twelve years ago, a bunch of us girls were sitting around on a Saturday morning watching TV. It had been a big night out at the bars the night before, and we had no plans of accomplishing anything that day except to order pizza and nurse our hangovers. All of the sudden a commercial came on the television advertising an air and holiday package to Hawaii.

With three weeks left in the semester, this looked very tempting. Of course, we were college students and none of us had any money. One of the girls said, "We should do that! I can charge the package on my credit card and the rest of you can buy tickets and come out. We could live there for the summer and get jobs." I don't know if it was our weakened state of mind or just our sense of adventure, but it didn't take much before we were all on the phones with our charge cards in hand. We arrived in Maui three weeks later to find out that the holiday unit advertised in the package was really just a studio apartment. I learned more that summer about girlfriends than you could possibly imagine. We were able to upgrade to a one bedroom after a week. I spent my summer in this one-bedroom apartment with eight other girls. You can probably guess that we became pretty close—in more ways than one. I had grown up living with brothers and was not used to sharing clothes, make up, boys, and so on. This all changed pretty quickly. Within the first week, I learned that "what's mine is yours." Mostly I learned this by spending hours looking for a certain item and then later seeing it on one of the other girls at a club later that night. The camaraderie outweighed any of the challenges, and it was one of the best summers of my life.

One evening while we were all dining at a Mexican restaurant on the water, I learned one of life's big lessons on giving and friendship. Marie had a crush on one of the waiters at the restaurant, which was the main the reason we were dining there in the first place. After a few pitchers of margaritas and some dancing, a few of us rushed off to the bathroom. Marie looked distraught. I didn't understand this because she had been dancing with Devon all night and things looked as if they were going great. With a look of distress and a trembling upper lip, she blurted out that she was in big trouble. We all asked her why. She told us that Devon had asked her to go home with him and that she was wearing her granny panties. At that instant, she pulled down her skirt and showed us her underwear, like a second grader under the slide at recess. We all laughed and agreed that there was no way she could go home with him that night. She then looked as us and exclaimed, "What have you got?" Most of us were thrown back by the situation but her two best friends, Ann and Colleen, didn't hesitate. Colleen had on some brand new pink lacy panties and was happy to exchange them with Marie. The whole bunch of us was in hysterics as we left the bathroom. I knew that instant that I had learned a very important lesson in friendship: there is no such thing as going too far to help out a friend in need.

This is just one example of a situation where a girlfriend would do whatever it took to help a friend. I learned over the years that this was just the tip of the iceberg when it comes to true friendship. I have been blessed during my life to have some of the most amazing girlfriends in the world. Some of these friendships are just pure good luck, and some of them are because I would literally do anything for any one of my friends. Life can sometimes present challenging experiences, and, if you have wonderful girlfriends that you can depend on, it will make your journey much simpler.

It was a Sunday night. All was quiet in our San Francisco flat where I lived with three of my best friends. I was going through a miserable breakup with my boyfriend of three years. I couldn't sleep; sleep now seemed foreign to me. I was not able to fight off the urge to call him just to hear his voice. It was forbidden in our house for me to make any sort of contact with him after my friends saw how sad I was about the breakup. But now everyone was asleep, and nobody would know the difference. I just needed to hear his voice. I anxiously grabbed the phone and dialed his number. Big mistake. He was at a dinner in a fancy restaurant. I asked him who he was with, and he told me he was with his mother and his best friend. He asked if it would be OK to call me later and I agreed.

Little did he know he hadn't hung up his cell phone. I thought he had seemed a bit flustered and had gotten off the phone in a hurry. I quickly learned why. He had been hiding the fact that he had a new girlfriend only weeks after the breakup. This was the big night, three weeks after our breakup, that he was going to introduce her to his mother. This was an incredibly painful conversation to overhear because I was unaware of the new girlfriend and very close with his mother. I knew I should have hung up the phone right then, but he had been lying to me and I wanted to know the truth. I listened as she entered the restaurant and introductions were made. At that point I was in uncontrollable tears and ran down the hall to Marie's room with the phone in hand. She was dead asleep because she had a very important meeting the next morning. She immediately asked me what was wrong. With my hand safely over the mute button, I handed the phone off to her. She listened for about fifteen minutes, giving me the play-by-play of the situation. It was a horrible experience to go through, but the sight of her translating the situation and matching my anger gave an air of comedy to the situation.

The rest of the evening was spent with Marie sharing horrible dating experiences that she had been through and what she had learned from them. This made me feel a whole lot better because she was in a healthy relationship, and I really valued her opinion. It gave me a sense of strength and support to hear that she had been through a similar situation.

Girlfriends can also be an excellent source of learning through your life and relationships. They know you intimately and can offer invaluable advice while you are going through the trials and tribulations of going through hard times in life, finding Mr. Right, and having babies. They will be there to support you through heartbreaks and to celebrate your successes. There is nothing better than being able to call someone who knows you better than you know yourself to ask for advice in challenging situations.

During college I hung around a very large group of girls. Each night we went out to the bars, there would be fifteen to twenty of us all decked out and ready to have a great time. The majority of us were dating men from the same fraternity. We were known as the PITAs (the pains in the ass) because, once we got to the bar, trouble always broke out. Whether it was a disagreement between a couple or one of us spotting someone's boyfriend talking to another girl, it was always something.

In one semester, many of these relationships ended for various reasons. It was a semester full of sadness, and the house I lived in became somewhat of a heartbreak hotel. Anytime we got news of a couple splitting up, all the girls would gather at our house to offer support. The day usually started with the girl in tears telling her story. Then we would all chime in on how he was bad news in the first place. The rest of the afternoon was usually spent with periods of teary stories interspersed with periods of laughter. We would play the Whitney Houston *Bodyguard* song and laugh and cry until we got it all out. Although this was a painful experience, it was also very therapeutic. We created a bond that couldn't be duplicated. We created a support network so strong, it lasted through the next few difficult weeks as the girls dealt with the grief and challenges of ending the relationship. When I went through those difficult times, I learned something very important from my friends: there is nothing stronger than the bond that you have with your girlfriends. They will always be there for you to lend support. Friendship is one of life's greatest joys. There are certain things that you can only get from a girlfriend.

The next few years brought some challenging times for me. My mother became very ill and passed away. I went through a devastating breakup of a three-year relationship. No matter what happened, no matter what was going on, the girls were there for me. I highly recommend taking the time out to appreciate your friendships that you have in your life.

Friendships with your girlfriends can also be an excellent way to find strength in yourself and in each other. So many times women get into a relationship and they expect their men to be everything for them. They become too dependent on them. These women don't realize that there are some inherent differences between men and women and that men can't always provide everything a woman needs. When women are able to understand this and utilize their girlfriends for these situations, it will strengthen their relationships. This can be good for a relationship in many ways. First of all, it allows you to process many of the different things that go on. Sometimes as women, we just want to vent or get things off our chest. Men are different in this way. When a woman is complaining about things, she may feel better when she is done, but the man feels awful. He often feels like he has failed because his woman is not happy. He also may feel like he is responsible to fix the situation. When women use each other to vent and share their experiences, it is a win-win situation for everyone involved. We are usually able to come up with our own solutions to problems when we talk about them out loud. The other positive aspect in this situation is that women are typically much more compassionate and understanding of the need to vent than men are. I know I have often become frustrated after sharing certain information with a male partner when I felt like venting. Usually I get one of two responses: either he feels that the information I am sharing is stupid, or he offers me a solution to the problem. Neither one of us gets the outcome we are looking for, and both of us end up frustrated by the situation.

Girlfriends are also invaluable for sharing information. In life we are faced with many different circumstances. There is nothing better than being able to ask a girlfriend you trust about a situation you are concerned about. This can be anything from a behavior that you have noticed about your romantic partner to something that you wouldn't feel comfortable talking to anyone else about. I can't tell you how many times I have been sitting around with the girls and a topic, such as sexual positions, has come up. At first I have been hesitant to even join the conversation because it was a bit uncomfortable. After a while, I have found myself engrossed in the conversation and learning things about which I have always been curious. As we are maturing and going through different phases of life, having girlfriends that you can relate to can be extremely important. For example, many of my girlfriends have had babies in the last few years. They are an invaluable resource as to what I can expect when I have children. I am able to ask them specific, detailed questions about the pregnancy, labor, birth, and after-effects that I wouldn't even feel comfortable asking my doctor. The point is, your girlfriends can be an invaluable wealth of information.

It is common for some women to abandon their girlfriends when they enter into a new romantic relationship. This is a dangerous practice and one that I do not recommend. In order to have a successful relationship, it is necessary to have relationships with your girlfriends. This is a huge generalization, but men often have more work obligations or extracurricular activities that take them away from home. When girls bond together and spend time together, it can be healthy and fun, not just for the girls but for their partners too. One of the keys to a successful relationship is a happy, healthy woman. The more needs that you fulfill without having to depend on your partner, the better off you will be.

Girlfriends are also fun. You can do so many different things with your girlfriends. One suggestion is to expand your comfort zone. Take a stripping or exotic massage class. Plan a scheduled girls' night out each week. Start a book club or a women's support group. Obviously, I am passionate about the importance of girlfriends in our lives. Girlfriends are an amazing gift of love, support, and companionship that we can give ourselves. Make this a priority in your life and you too will see the benefits.

9

Dating Yourself First

There is nothing more attractive than a woman who is happy, self-assured, busy, and fulfilled.

My first Valentine's Day with John proved to be a bit disappointing. He had been the most amazing boyfriend up until then. On my birthday, he had surprised me at work with a dozen roses and a chocolate cake for the entire office. Then, I arrived home after being sent out for a massage to find my apartment filled with balloons and presents. Let's just say I had high hopes for this special holiday. I was on the road for business, and he was at his home in Australia. I pretty much planted every seed I could in hopes for something special to come my way. I even had the time change in my favor. Because Australia is across the International Date Line, it was Valentine's Day there the day before it was in America. I called him that morning and let him know how happy I was that he was my valentine. I thought for sure that even if he had forgotten entirely about the special day, this would at least give him time to send a fax, an e-mail, flowers, or something. He said he was happy that I was his valentine too. That was pretty much the extent of the festivities.

The next day came and went, and I watched as other girls received roses and gifts from their men. I tried to reassure myself that it was OK because we had such an amazing relationship and that it didn't matter. The truth was that I was pretty bummed about the whole thing. When he called later that evening, I expressed my disappointment. He justified his actions by saying that he showed me his extraordinary love every day of the year and didn't want to feel like he had to do something just because it was a holiday. He was right; he did do a great job expressing his love for me. I fell asleep feeling much better and very loved.

The next day while I was shopping at a local high end grocery store, I couldn't help noticing that there were some of the most beautiful roses that I had ever seen left over from Valentine's Day. Suddenly it dawned on me. I was loved and there was no reason at all for me to feel bad. I grabbed one of the beautiful bouquets of roses and put it into my basket. My girlfriend asked me what I was doing, and I told her I had a brilliant idea. It was then that I came up with the concept of "dating yourself." I took those roses home, arranged them in a beautiful vase, and gave them water. I told myself that they were from my boyfriend at the time, at least symbolically. The next time he called I let him know what I had done and let him know he owed me $25.00 for the flowers. He laughed because I was always up to something silly. The act of getting the roses myself proved to be much more important than if I had received them from him.

I realized that day that, whether you are in a relationship or not, it is extremely important to continue to nurture yourself with all of the wonderful things that usually accompany a new relationship. From that day forward, I made sure to schedule out special time for myself—a date night, so to speak. I will give you many examples of how to do this, but, in general, remember to find the practices that make you feel good and build your self-confidence.

The first practice I developed in dating yourself is a romantic evening. The hustle and bustle of everyday life can get cumbersome, and sometimes we forget how good it can feel to spoil ourselves. I make it a practice of having romantic dinners for myself from time to time. When things get busy or stressful or when I miss my boyfriend, I schedule one of these dinners. I start by going to the local specialty supermarket and shopping for my dinner. Upon entering the store, I have the same sensation I do when shopping for a hot date, and I usually shop with a huge smile on my face. When I began this practice, I lived alone, so it was easy to make time for special dinners. However, if you want to do this with a girlfriend or roommate, that would work fine too. Make sure you buy everything you would if you were preparing a meal for a significant other. I start with candles and a beautiful bunch of flowers. From there, I visit the deli and select a beautiful piece of fish. Then I choose the proper complements, such as vegetables and rice or pasta. Then on to the selection of a nice bottle of wine that will complement the chosen meal. After that is all done, I select the most decadent dessert possible from the bakery. I pull out all the stops. There is no calorie counting on these evenings. I go home and create romantic ambience in my apartment, as if I were waiting for my lover to come dine with me. The simple act of preparing everything makes me feel wonderful. Once everything is ready, I savor my dinner slowly, listening to love songs on the radio or to my favorite CD. This romantic night is a wonderful way to remind yourself that you deserve the best.

I mentioned flowers above. They are actually the reason I invented the concept of dating yourself. Everyone has experienced a time in their lives when they have received flowers either at work or at the start of a date. For some reason, this simple gesture can make a women feel so special and loved. I realized that you don't need a man in your life to achieve these same feelings. I recommend buying yourself flowers weekly. It makes the days go by easier when you have a lovely arrangement of flowers to look at. You can purchase them for your workplace, which usually invokes curiosity from others; many people will ask who sent you the flowers. Or you may prefer to have them delivered to your home. I recommend buying a bunch that is traditionally perceived as romantic, such as roses or orchids. This adds an air of romance to your work or living space.

Spa dates are another great way to pamper yourself. This can be done at home or in an elegant spa. Since this is one of my favorite activities in life, I would recommend taking advantage of both. It is fairly simple to give yourself a luxurious spa treatment at home. It is important that you schedule this time just as you would a date. If you have a bathtub, creating a romantic bubble bath for yourself can be truly rewarding. The key here, just as it was with the romantic dinner, is to create the same environment you would if you were preparing a romantic bath for your lover. Create an ambience of romance by using candles, essential oils, bubble bath, and rose petals. When you are ready, slide into the bath with romantic music in the background and enjoy an evening of indulgence. It is nice to bring in a refreshing drink. My personal favorite is a glass of sparkling water with a slice of lime in a wineglass. Trust me, after such an evening you will feel extremely pampered and loved. Another way you can spoil yourself is to book a treatment at your local spa. Most cities have many different spas from which to choose. It can be a fun hobby to try out different spas each time and have a variety of experiences. This activity can be enjoyed by yourself or with a girlfriend. The outcome is to spoil yourself and make yourself feel decadent.

Writing a love letter to yourself is another great tool in dating yourself. This is a simple practice that, when done regularly, can remind you what an amazing person you are and how much you deserve to be loved. It is helpful to set a romantic ambience when you are writing a love letter to yourself. Burn some incense or essential oils. Make sure you have some romantic stationery and plenty of candles burning. Play a favorite love song as you begin to write down all of the things that you admire and love about yourself. You can write out how you would feel if you were in a relationship, or, if you are currently in a relationship, you can write out all of the things you are proud of. These can be kept in a special box somewhere in your home for you to access whenever you feel like reminiscing or you need a boost of encouragement.

Pink! It is really important that you have many different items in both your environment and your wardrobe that make you feel feminine. I have a running joke when I do the laundry: I am washing my darks, whites, or pinks. Over the last few years I have discovered the value of having bright, feminine colors to wear and how much they affect your mood. For many, many years my wardrobe was mostly black and earthy tones. I didn't realize the power of owning a number of pink items. When I wear pink I notice an immediate difference in the way I feel. Another great bonus of wearing pink is that I receive compliments daily. (Let's face it, ladies: who doesn't want to be told how great they look each day?) It's interesting that the comments I receive usually have to do with the clothing item being feminine or sexy. The color of your clothes is a little thing that can make a big difference.

Getting dressed up just as you would for a date is another practice that I highly recommend in dating yourself. So many times when women aren't in a relationship and they aren't out looking for someone, they forget what it feels like to get dressed for a hot date or a big night out on the town. This is especially important when you are single; it can help you attract people into your life. There is truth in the saying, "You look good, you feel good." I recommend getting dressed up at least once a week. This is not to say that the rest of the time you are sitting at home in sweats, but really get gussied up like it is a special occasion. It can feel amazing to get dressed in your fancy clothes with fine fabrics like silk and lace. Just the act of selecting and purchasing fine nylons will make you feel good about yourself. Pull out all of the stops! Make sure to take extra time primping your hair and applying makeup. Perhaps you should choose a lipstick that is brighter and more vivacious than you are used to. Of course this night can be combined with your romantic dinner or your love letter, or you may chose to hit the town and meet a girlfriend for drinks. Don't be surprised if you find yourself fighting off the men. Spending extra time and energy making yourself look and feel good will cause you to radiate a different energy than usual.

Sexy lingerie is a must when you are dating yourself. Get rid of the granny panties and your comfy underwear. There is no place for them. I can't tell you how many times I have been in a lingerie store and heard a woman say, "It's not like anyone else is going to see them." This is not the point. I believe that lingerie is just as much for yourself as it is for your partner, if not more. Even if you have no plans at all of letting anyone else see you in your lingerie, it can be extremely powerful in making you feel sexy and attractive. Here is a little challenge for you: I encourage you to wear sexy lingerie every day for a week under your regular clothes. I guarantee you that this alone will give you a whole different perception of yourself, and it will give off a different energy to others. I have a girlfriend that I travel with that taught me this trick. It is not unheard of that we will be waiting for a bus somewhere, in weather cold enough to be snowing, and one of us will laugh as we readjust some part of the lingerie that is under our winter clothes.

The last tool that I want to give you is flirting. Flirting is essential, even when you are in a relationship. I have taught numerous women all over the world an excellent flirting strategy. It is very simple. All you need to do is find a local coffee shop that is located near a professional business area. This shouldn't be too terribly difficult to do. Identify what time the businessmen come in to get their coffee, and make sure you align your schedule to get yours at the same time. The rest will take care of itself. All you need to do is flash a pearly white smile and you will be bombarded with flirting. I recommend this activity even if you are in a relationship; it is harmless and it can help you boost your self-esteem and make you feel desirable. I used to make it my mission to have some sort of interaction each morning while I was getting coffee. This could be as simple as having someone open the door for me when I arrived or striking up a conversation while I was putting milk in my coffee. It is a great way to learn how to communicate with the opposite sex in a nonthreatening environment.

If you complete these activities on a regular basis, you will give yourself the self-confidence to attract anything you desire into your life.

10

Life Is a Precious Gift

Life must be lived forward and understood backward.

About four years ago, I found myself in Australia with a work assignment. I was traveling with about twelve other amazing people from all over the world. It was such a blessing to be exposed to a multicultural group. We were there for a seminar and then would conduct coaching sessions with the participants from the event. We were staying in beautiful, pristine Coogee beach. One of the mornings there would be a team building exercise on the cliffs overlooking the sea, at the top of the beach. This was right up my alley.

The morning of the team building exercise, we strolled down the beautiful beachfront streets. There was an air of anticipation; we were the only early risers, with the exception of a lone jogger here and there. The air was crisp, and smelled faintly of sea and dew. All of the restaurants and shops were shut down, and I could almost feel the lingering energy from the hustle and bustle from the night before.

The beaches were clean and calm with waves crashing along the shoreline. I remember thinking to myself that the ocean is such an amazingly powerful specimen. It has the ability to be magical and beautiful and at the same time so powerful. It can provide vacationers with endless joy and entertainment as they splash in the waves all day. It can also provide food with its supply of fish and provide sport to so many. It has existed for thousands and thousands of years, and its pure existence is a treasure to see.

The cliffs ahead were magnificent. They were sandstone with a hint of red in the rock. They looked as though they had been created from centuries of erosion. It was impossible to believe that the water would have ever stretched that far. As we approached the cliffs, a sense of warmth began to radiate within my body, and I had the feeling that this was someplace special. Not only did this place have majestic beauty; this was truly a spiritual place.

While taking in this magical beauty, we assembled in a circle and took our seats. Then the sun begun to rise, providing the smallest bit of warmth and shedding light on even more beauty. One of the men in the group had brought his guitar and began to play and sing a song that he had written. It was truly a special experience. While we enjoyed the music, we were given instructions for our assignment: we were to write out everything that we had accomplished over the last few years and everything we were proud of. It was an excellent exercise; so many times we move through life so quickly that we don't stop to appreciate our successes.

At first I began to ponder. It is difficult to think offhand of things that deserve acknowledgment. I looked around at the group, and everyone was engrossed in their assignment. Then it dawned on me. The last few years had been different from any others in my life.

A few years back my mother had become very ill and was hospitalized. She remained in the hospital for three months as she rapidly deteriorated. It was tragic to watch her worsen day after day, barely clinging to life at times. The next three months were filled with days spend at the hospital, from sunup to sundown, much of it spent dealing with doctors and bureaucracy. My family did everything possible to try to make the days more comfortable and pain free for my mother, knowing that this would be the last precious time we would spent together. After three long and grueling months, my mother passed away. I was able to be there with her when it happened and literally held her hand during the process. She was surrounded by family and everyone that loved her. At the time, the process seemed surreal. It was like something I had seen on television with all of the monitors and doctors and the way it happens, yet at the same time so powerful and painful that I knew deep down that her death would shift the very person that I was.

My mother had very powerful spiritual beliefs regarding the afterlife, and I knew from that day forward she would be a powerful guardian angel and watch over my every move in life. When you lose someone close to you, everyone in your life has concerns over your well-being. They assume you must be angry or feel cheated that this happened to you. I felt quite the contrary. The evening of her memorial service, I mentioned to my friends that all I wanted to do was to help others who were going though the same type of experience.

As this experience and all the thoughts surrounding it swirled around in my head, I put pen to paper. I wrote madly about how this experience had changed my life and that I was given the gift of not taking things too seriously and appreciating each and every second, as no one knows when it will end. It freed me from the stresses of daily life and liberated me from the rat race. I had an instantaneous shift in values and a new outlook on life. I was given the ability to love more deeply and completely, an intuitive sense to understand the world differently, and compassion for understanding others' behaviors. This concept was larger than I could understand at twenty-three, and something that would continue to grow, flourish, and prosper.

As the beautiful music came to an end, a woman's voice said that our time for the exercise was over. It was time to share what we had written and to allow others to acknowledge us for our accomplishments. I had such a sense of inner peace and well-being. It was such a sense of contentment that I almost didn't want to share what I had written. In the same thought, I knew that my lesson was an amazing and powerful one and that it was part of my purpose in life to spread this message.

The sharing of everyone's successes turned out to be a powerful experience. I was blessed to be traveling with an extraordinary group of people; each person had accomplished amazing things. Some people had been through powerful experiences and tragedies, and it was beautiful to watch the group lend support and love to the reader. When it came time to share mine, I felt a nervousness shoot through my body. I had an inner knowing that this gift I had been given would probably be the most powerful of my entire life. I had to clear my throat and fight back the tears. They weren't tears of sadness, rather tears of joy and exuberance knowing I had learned one of life's secrets early on and was ready to share it with others. As I read through my list of accomplishments, I could sense others becoming equally emotional. Through my writing I was able to share this lesson and teach others the preciousness of life.

When I finished reading and looked up, the sun was beaming and glistening off the water. I felt as though it was a little wink of reassurance from heaven that I was in the right place and on the right path. All was well.

Another very important moment happened for me on that rock. One of the girls on the team had shared that her mother had recently been diagnosed with cancer. She shared some of the lessons she was learning and the difficulties that are associated with this. After we were done reading, I went over, gave her a hug, and let her know I would always be there to support her if she needed anything. At the time I had just recently met this woman but felt a tremendous connection with her.

The years went by, and the angels intervened. This woman, Amber, became one of my very best friends and someone who will remain in my life forever. Unfortunately, her mother did pass on. I felt honored to be there to lend support and help her through this difficult time. The beautiful and amazing part of the story is that she shared very much the same experience and belief system that I did and felt that she had been given such a gift to appreciate each and every moment in life. We often joke about our moms being up in Heaven, throwing parties and looking down on us while they arrange different occurrences in our lives.

Four years later, Amber and I found ourselves in Australia for another work assignment. We knew that life had brought us together in this place, and we had to make another pilgrimage to the cliffs at Coogee Beach. We planned our adventure for a Friday evening. We were staying in downtown Sydney and had to take a twenty-minute cab ride to the beloved beach town. On the way there, I felt the anticipation build. So much had happened since that morning four years ago. Life had taken so many unexpected turns and twists, and it was incredible to revisit all that had occurred.

Our first stop was at a lovely Italian restaurant. We were going to celebrate life and have an incredible dinner to honor our rituals that evening. We didn't spare anything; we enjoyed the finest wine, appetizers, entrees, and our favorite white chocolate crème brûlée for dessert.

After the festivities were finished, we headed down to the beach and up toward the rocks. We ventured down the same street we had four years ago. This time the streets were alive with energy. All of the outdoor seating was filled with tourists and diners who were enjoying this special place.

As we made our way down to the beach, we could hear the waves crashing on the sand. The scenery was much different at night, but you didn't have to see the actual landscape to appreciate its majestic beauty. We began the climb to our sacred spot and found the perfect place for us to sit. This would prove to be one of the most special evenings of my life.

We had brought with us lists of what we wanted to release in our lives and what we wanted to attract. We lit the candles and incense we had brought with us and even had some vabotti from Sai Baba, which we placed on our third eye. I went first. I read all of the things in my life that I wanted to release. This included emotions, feelings, and patterns. When I had completed the list, I stood up. Amber brushed my entire body with some white sage we were burning. We both set the intention that this would be released from my life as I ripped up the paper, burned it, and threw the ashes off the cliff. We repeated the exercise with her list and followed the same routine with the intentions and the white sage. As I watched her throw her list, now ash, off the cliffs, I realized how powerful this activity was. The experiences I had had at these cliffs years before had proven to be so magical. We then took turns with our lists of what we wanted to attract into our lives. These lists were much longer and with each item that was read, we celebrated as if we already had this in our lives. When we finished reading our lists, we lit a sparkler in celebration of what was ahead in our lives.

Then we played an incredible game. Amber called it "remembering forward." We spent the next two hours "remembering" all of the things we wanted in our lives. At first it seemed a bit silly and superficial, but as the game got going, it took on a life of its own. We told stories of remembering the day our children we wanted were born and the funny circumstances that happened. We remembered our first dinner party with Nelson Mandela and Oprah there as guests. We remembered the day our books hit the best-seller list and we were on *The View*. The game went on for hours. We would laugh hysterically, as we joined each other in memories and added details only a great friend could know.

The funny thing was that a part of me really felt as though all of that had happened in our lives. I felt so attached to all of our "pretend" memories that I could feel what it would be like the day they actually will happen. It was a profound experience and one we revisit frequently in conversations.

Your exercise for this chapter is simple. Remember forward. You can do this alone or with a trusted friend. Write out everything you desire in the next few years and then speak about it as if it has already happened. The more detailed and specific you are the more associated you will become and the quicker you will manifest this into your life.

Remember, life is short; you never know how many special moments you have left. Treasure each of them and live a life full of richness and happiness. You deserve the best. You are "the one."

Now you have everything you need to attract and nurture your ideal dream life. I want to acknowledge you for taking the time and energy to work on these very important areas of your life. I wish you the best of luck in your journey and would love to hear about your successes. I am available for one-on-one coaching throughout your journey. To share your successes and for more information, please visit www.theonecoaching.com. Thank you for allowing me to pass on the wisdom I have learned from women all over the world. Here's to a wonderful journey!

"The One" Coaching Program

"The One" coaching program is available to women who are looking to learn how to manifest excellence in their lives, whether in relationships, health, careers, or anything else.

The coaching program consists of a ten-week series that follows the same principles as this best-selling book. This coaching is excellent for women who are looking to attract something special into their lives as well as for women who are currently in a relationship, in a successful career, and in great health and looking to improve their experience.

Through the coaching, you will experience a journey that provides you answers in the areas of acceptance, discovering you purpose, identifying your unsupportive patterns from your past, and much more. You will learn how to create strategies to design and attract anything you desire into your life.

This coaching program will not only allow you to attract amazing relationships, careers, health, and vitality, it will also show you how to create abundance in all areas of your life.

Currently Bonnie, the author, is traveling around the world, coaching and mentoring for one of the world's leading personal development speakers, as well as running "The One" coaching. There are limited spaces for "The One" coaching. If you feel this program is right for you, please contact Bonnie at www.theonecoaching.com.

bonnie@theonecoaching.com

About the Author

Bonnie Bruderer grew up in Marin County, California. She attended California State University, Chico, where she received a BA in journalism and a minor in sociology. She went on to receive a holistic health practitioner degree from the School of Healing Arts in San Diego. She is a leading innovator and expert on coaching women on how to create abundance in their lives. With her holistic background, experience as a coach and mentor, and life experiences, she has created an easy-to-read book with powerful exercises that can guide any woman toward what it is she truly desires.

Bonnie is the creator of "The One" coaching. "The One" is a coaching program in which a coach and mentor guides you through each of the necessary steps to create abundance in all areas of your life and attract amazing relationships.

Bonnie currently spends half of her time traveling around the world with the world's leading personal development speaker as a coach and mentor. When she is not on the road, she spends her time in Mill Valley running a busy wellness center. She has coached hundreds of people into the life of their dreams in five different countries.

In her free time, Bonnie enjoys spending time with her many cherished girlfriends and family, yoga (both teaching and practicing), vegan cooking, and competing in triathlons. She completed her first Ironman Triathlon in March 2003.

Her life's purpose is to inspire women around the world to radiate and to live the lives of their dreams.

For further information on "The One" coaching programs, visit www.theonecoaching.com.

978-0-595-37863-0
0-595-37863-3

Printed in the United States
46136LVS00003B/7-159